and the Making of the Modern World

ALAN MACFARLANE

2018

CAM RIVERS PUBLISHING

First published in Great Britain in 2018

5 Canterbury Close
Cambridge CB4 3QQ

www.cambridgerivers.com
press@cambridgerivers.com

Author: Alan Macfarlane
Series Editor: Zilan Wang
Editor: Sarah Harrison
Marketing Manager: James O'Sullivan
Typesetting and cover design: Jaimie Norman

The publication of this book has been supported by
the Kaifeng Foundation.

© Alan Macfarlane, 2018

The moral right of the author
has been asserted.

All rights reserved. Without limiting the rights under copyright reserved above, no part of this publication may be reproduced, stored or introduced into a retrieval system, or transmitted, in any form or by any means (electronic, mechanical, photocopying, recording or otherwise), without prior written permission of both the copyright owner and publisher of this book.

Contents

	Acknowledgements	*v*
	Note on References, Conventions and Measures	*vi*
	Abbreviated titles of works by Adam Smith	*viii*
	Preface	1
1.	Adam Smith's Life and Work	3
2.	Growth and Stasis	25
3.	Of Wealth and Liberty	47
4.	From Predation to Production	70
	Bibliography	104

Acknowledgements

As with all books, this is a composite work and I would like to thank some of the many people who have helped me on the way to completing it. Andrew Morgan and Harry Pitt, former teachers, originally inspired me with an interest in the Enlightenment. Penny Lang typed, checked, and commented on numerous versions of the text. Iris Macfarlane read the text several times. John Davey read the typescript twice and was his usual encouraging and wise self. Cecilia Scurrah Ehrhart carefully checked the footnotes. Lily Harrison Blakely through her birth gave me inspiration.

To these I would like to add the University of Tokyo, and in particular Professor Takeo Funabiki, which funded a sabbatical term during which, among other things, I re-wrote sections of the text. Marilyn Strathern for, once again, shielding me from administrative pressures and for wise leadership. To Cherry Bryant for reading and checking the text several times. And to my friends on the internet, Gabriel Andrade, Michael Lotus, Jim Bennett and James McCormick for all their advice and support.

My greatest thanks I reserve to the end. Gerry Martin has over the years been a constant source of support and inspiration. He read the whole text several times and we discussed it at length. The first few pages of the book are taken directly from his own writing. In many ways this is a collaborative work with him. Also I thank Hilda Martin for her friendship, encouragement and support. Finally, Sarah Harrison has, as always, given enormous help in every possible way, including several constructive readings of the text which helped to shorten it by a quarter. This book is likewise a collaborative work with her.

References, Conventions and Measures

NORMALLY, MUCH OF the materials in a monograph would be one's own. This book, however, is a work in which I try to let Tocqueville speak to us in his own words. Consequently it is a patchwork of quotations with a concomitant effect on style. On the other hand I hope that the authenticity of the chosen authors will enrich the argument.

Spelling has not been modernized. American spelling (e.g. labor for labour) has usually been changed to the English variant. Italics in quotations are in the original, unless otherwise indicated. Variant spellings in quotations have not been corrected.

Round brackets in quotations are those of the original author; my interpolations are in square brackets. In the quotations from Adam Smith, where angled brackets have been used by modern editors to show where words or letters have been added, I have reproduced these. Square brackets are used for my interpolations or expansions.

The footnote references give an abbreviated title and page number. The usual form is author, short title, volume number if there is one (in upper case Roman numerals), page number(s). The full title of the work referred to is given in the bibliography at the end of the book, where there is also a list of common abbreviations used in the footnotes.

Where several quotations within a single paragraph are taken from the same author, the references are given after the last of the quotations. Each page reference is given, even if it is a repeated page number.

Measures

A number of the quotations refer to English systems of measurement, some of which are now no longer in use.

Value: four farthings to a penny, twelve pennies (d) to a shilling (s), twenty shillings to a pound (£). One pound in the seventeenth century was worth about 40 times its present value (in 1997).

Weight: sixteen ounces to a pound, fourteen pounds to a stone, eight stone to hundred-weight (cwt) and twenty hundred-weight to a ton. (approx one pound (lb) equals 0.454 kg).

Liquid volume: two pints to a quart, four quarts to a gallon (approx one and three quarter pints to one litre).

Distance: twelve inches to a foot, three feet to a yard, 1760 yards to a mile. (approx 39.4 inches to 1 metre).

Area: an acre. (approx 2.47 acres to a hectare).

Abbreviated titles of books by Adam Smith (1723-90)

Moral The   *Theory of Moral Sentiments* (1759), George Bell, 1907

Wealth   *An Inquiry into the Nature and Causes of the Wealth of Nations* (1775), 2 vols in 1, Univ. of Chicago Press paperback edn., 1976

Philosophical *Essays on Philosophical Subjects*, Indianapolis, 1982

Jurisprudence *Lectures on Jurisprudence*, Indianapolis, 1982

Rhetoric   *Lectures of Rhetoric and Belles Lettres*, Indianapolis, 1985

Correspondence *Correspondence of Adam Smith*, Indianapolis, 1987

Preface

My book *The Riddle of the Modern World; Of Liberty, Wealth and Equality* was published by Macmillan in 2000. It discussed the work of four major writers who had dedicated their lives to trying to answer the riddle of how our modern world originated and what its future might be. These were the Baron de Montesquieu (1689-1755), Adam Smith (1723-90), Alexis de Tocqueville (1805-59) and Ernest Gellner (1920-95).

The book was modestly successful and went into paperback. Yet, by combining these thinkers, the distinctive contribution of each one may have been somewhat muffled. This long and quite expensive book did not reach a wider audience who might be potentially interested in one or two of the authors treated, but not all of them at once.

So I have decided to re-issue each part as a downloadable electronic book, and add others parts of my exploration of the riddle of modernity in due course, including the assessment of a number of other key thinkers such as F.W.Maitland and Yukichi Fukuzawa.

Apart from correcting a few minor errors I have not otherwise altered the text of this section on Smith. Since I wrote the original chapters some ten years ago, there has been further work on the problems which Smith and the other thinkers I have written about addressed. To have incorporated this more recent work would have created a different book. I hope one day to consider this new work in a wider appraisal of not only Smith but of my whole attempt to pursue the 'riddle of the world', which will also incorporate the final synthetic chapter to *The Riddle of the Modern World*, 'The Riddle Resolved?', which is omitted here.

I subsequently lectured on Smith and other thinks for second year students at Cambridge University. The filmed lecture can be seen at:

www.alanmacfarlane.com/theorists/smith.htm

I particularly enjoyed giving this lecture since I feel that Smith provided a very penetrating answer to many of the puzzles relating to the origins and nature of the modern world. His work has also been enormously influential and still guides the way in which many people think. I present my assessment of his contribution to these wide questions with no further introduction since I believe that his brilliant speculations stand on their own merits. It is obvious what problems he is addressing and many of his insights are still relevant today.

ONE

Adam Smith's Life and Work

THE HISTORIAN H.A.L. Fisher summarized the life and influence of Adam Smith as follows:

> A Scot by birth and descent and mixing with the skippers and merchants of Glasgow, where he was long a Professor, he caught the temper of a great seaport struggling against fiscal fetters. His **Wealth of Nations** (1776), the Bible of Economic Science, states in powerful and measured terms the case for Freedom of Trade, and has long governed British policy. Pitt the younger, Huskisson, Peel, Gladstone, Asquith were his pupils. The soul of modesty.[1]

Adam Smith was born in 1723 in Kirkcaldy on the Firth of Forth in Scotland, the son of a Judge Advocate and Comptroller of Customs in the port. His father died just before he was born and he was brought up by his widowed mother. He went to Kirkcaldy grammar school and then in 1737 to Glasgow University where he obtained an M.A. in 1740. In that year he went to Balliol College, Oxford, remaining there for six years. After returning to Scotland he spent two years with his mother and then lived in Edinburgh from 1748 to 1751 where he gave public lectures on literature and jurisprudence. It was at this time that he began what was to become a deep friendship with the philosopher David Hume. Smith was elected Professor of Logic and then Professor of Moral Philosophy at the University of Glasgow

---

1 On a printed postcard at the front of the King's College, Cambridge copy of Fay, **Adam Smith**

where he lived from 1751 to 1763. He published his **Theory of Moral Sentiments** in 1759.

In 1764 Smith went to France as tutor of the Duke of Buccleugh and remained there until 1766. He met many of the greatest philosophers and political economists. After a brief stay in London he returned to Kirkcaldy in 1767 and remained there almost without a break until April 1773, working on drafts of **The Wealth of Nations**. He then moved to London and spent a further two and a half years revising the manuscript which was published in 1776 to great acclaim. From 1778 until his death on July 17, 1790 he lived mainly in Edinburgh, employed as a Commissioner of Customs and the Salt Duty. Smith never married and his lifelong companions were his mother, who died in 1787 and his cousin Jane who died a year later.

It was during the years in Glasgow as a teacher and also an effective and conscientious administrator, that Smith laid the foundations for his great works. His experience in England had given him a geographical contrast between wealthy England and relatively poor Scotland, but his experience in Kirkcaldy and Glasgow between the 1730s and 1760s gave him an equally important temporal contrast. This was a perfect place from which to witness two dramatic changes. The first was the transformation of the political system. Up to 1745 the older world of the clan system and Catholicism still remained strong in the Highlands as a living contrast to the religious, political and social system of lowland Scotland and England. Then, while Smith was in Oxford, occurred the last attempt to re-impose this alternative world with the 1745 uprising. When Smith returned in 1746 it was to a country where the clan system was being systematically crushed in the aftermath to Culloden. Smith was thus living on the border of two civilizations and in his formative years watched one of them decisively defeat the other. His unusual insight into the deepest structures of commercial capitalism came out of this experience.

The development of Glasgow itself re-enforced this sense of a great shift. Part of the sense of living in two worlds is captured by W.R. Scott when he describes the Glasgow to which Smith returned as Professor of Moral Philosophy. 'The town was his laboratory. In the midst of the eighteenth century it was a remarkable blend of the old and the new. The history of the last hundred years had left enduring traces which were being modified slowly, and sometimes painfully, by new spirit and by new conditions.'[1] The rapid development of Glasgow in this period is excellently described by Rae, for

> *Glasgow had already begun its transition from the small provincial to the great commercial capital, and was therefore at a stage of development of special value to the philosophical observer. Though still only a quiet but picturesque old place, nestling about the Cathedral and the College and two fine but sleepy streets, in which carriers built their haystacks out before their door, it was carrying on a trade which was even then cosmopolitan. The ships of Glasgow were in all the waters of the world, and its merchants had won the lead in at least one important branch of commerce, the West India tobacco trade, and were founding fresh industries every year with the greatest possible enterprise.*[2]

Glasgow was a place where new worlds were being discovered and new methods tried. Smith spent a great deal of time observing and talking to the merchants and made many close friends among them, in particular, Andrew Cochrane, later Provost of Glasgow and described by Smollet as '"one of the first sages of the Scottish Kingdom."'[3] Cochrane was clearly a remarkable man;

---

1 Scott, **Smith**, 78
2 Rae, **Smith**, 88-9
3 Rae, **Smith**, 91

> *Dr. Carlyle tells that 'Dr. Smith acknowledged his obligations to this gentleman's information when he was collecting materials for his **Wealth of Nations**...' Dr. Carlyle informs us, more-over, that Cochrane founded a weekly club in the 'forties' - a political economy club - of which 'the express design was to inquire into the nature and principles of trade in all its branches, and to communicate knowledge and ideas on that subject to each other,' and that Smith became a member of this club after coming to reside in Glasgow.[1]*

Yet Adam Smith would not just have learnt about trade and merchant activities from his Glasgow friends, for there was also rapid industrial development. These new entrepreneurs

> *founded the Smithfield ironworks, and imported iron from Russia and Sweden to make hoes and spades for the negroes of Maryland. They founded the Glasgow tannery in 1742, which Pennant thought an amazing sight, and where they employed 300 men making saddles and shoes for the plantations. They opened the Pollokshaws linen printfield in 1742, copper and tin works in 1747, the Delffield pottery in 1748. They began to manufacture carpets and crape in 1759, silk in 1759, and leather gloves in 1763. They opened the first Glasgow bank - the Ship - in 1750, and the second - the Arms - in 1752. They first began to improve the navigation of the Clyde by the Act of 1759; they built a dry dock at their harbour of Port Glasgow in 1762; while in 1768 they deepened the Clyde up to the city, and began (for this also was mainly their work) the canal to the Forth for their trade with the Baltic. It was obvious, therefore, that this was a period of unique commercial enterprise and expansion.[2]*

Thus Adam Smith could see the world changing before his eyes and the affluence he had seen at Oxford spreading rapidly into Scotland. The shock for Smith was made more dramatic in that the very ten years when he had been absent

---

1 Rae, **Smith**, 90-1

2 Rae, **Smith**, 89

from Glasgow, 1740-1750, had witnessed 'a very great change in the appearance of the district. Looking down from the high ground near the University, recently completed mansions of merchants and others in the course of building came into view.'[3] He lived in a boom-town and watched a feudal, Calvinist, world dissolving into a commercial capitalist one. **The Wealth of Nations** is in many ways an almost autobiographical attempt to describe and explain how and why this was happening around him.

He was also living through a kind of experimental test of one of his major theories, namely that free trade and minimal governmental interference would allow the 'natural tendency' for wealth to increase.

> *When the eighteenth century began, Scotland was excluded, by a series of Acts of the English Legislature, from the Colonial trade. After the Union [in 1723], this restraint was removed, and, by every test, the advance in prosperity, particularly in the West, was remarkable, and even spectacular. Here, then, it seemed that there was something approaching a valid experiment for the verification of an hypothesis, and confirming it up to the hilt.*[4]

Smith was living just before the great textile and steam power boom of the later eighteenth century, or the growth of the heavy industries including building of steam ships that would give Glasgow its greatest reputation. This helps to explain certain absences in his work, in particular the omission of the importance of the steam engine. It is important to note this for another advantage of living in Glasgow and working in the University was that it was the home of several of those who would provide the scientific and technological basis for the industrial revolution. The sort of developments which were

---

3   Scott, **Smith**, 81
4   Scott, **Smith**, 114

happening along the corridor from Smith, and undertaken by friends of his, are described by Rae.

> *Only a few years before Smith's arrival they had recognised the new claims of science by establishing a chemical laboratory, in which during Smith's residence the celebrated Dr. Black was working out his discovery of latent heat. They gave a workshop in the College to James Watt in 1756, and made him mathematical instrument maker to the University, when the trade corporations of Glasgow refused to allow him to open a workshop in the city; and it was in that very workshop and at this very period that a Newcomen's engine he repaired set his thoughts revolving till the memorable morning in 1764 when the idea of the separate condenser leapt to his mind as he was strolling past the washhouse on Glasgow Green. They had at the same time in another corner of the College opened a printing office for the better advancement of that art, and were encouraging the University printer, the famous Robert Foulis, to print those Homers and Horaces by which he more than rivalled the Elzevirs and Etiennes of the past.*[1]

It is impossible to assess exactly what effect these exciting years in Glasgow had on Smith, but as we shall see, the surviving lecture notes suggest that he had worked out many of his theories to explain the central structural features of a modern commercial economy by 1763. As Stewart observed, 'His long residence in one of the most enlightened mercantile towns in this island, and the habits of intimacy in which he lived with the most respectable of its inhabitants, afforded him an opportunity of deriving what commercial information he stood in need of from the best sources.'[2] And at a deeper level, the contrasts which he could see in time and space, and the sheer rapidity of change, may be behind his great shift to a four-stage model of social development which Meek and others see as one of his greatest contributions. As Meek himself

---

1 Rae, **Smith**, 71
2 Stewart, **Works**, X, 42

suggests, it seems likely that it was 'the rapidity of contemporary economic advance' and the ease of contrasts between more and less advanced parts of Scotland and England, that gave him the clue. 'If changes in the mode of subsistence were playing such an important and "progressive" role in the development of contemporary society, it seemed a fair bet that they must also have done so in that of past society.'[3]

The situation in Glasgow and around Kirkcaldy was all the more impressive in comparison with the Highlands. As Ross points out 'Britain of the era of the '45 rising provided Smith with a contrast between the Highlands of Scotland at the pastoral stage with a warrior society and patriarchal leaders, and the unwarlike Lowlands, similar to England, organized for agriculture and commerce, and having to rely on a professional army for defence.'[4] Smith developed the theory that discovery and scientific advancement came out of the emotions of 'wonder' and 'surprise', and there was plenty to be amazed at in the Scotland of the 1750s.

Adam Smith had experienced the contrast between a prosperous commercial capitalism in England, and his own poorer Scottish background. This was one precipitant to thought. A second was the contrast within Europe. Early in 1764 having resigned his Professorship, he went to France as tutor of the Duke of Buccleuch, stepson and ward of Charles Townsend. He spent eighteen months in Toulouse and then 'About Christmas 1765, they returned to Paris, and remained there till October following. The society in which Mr. Smith spent those ten months, may be conceived from the advantages he enjoyed, in consequence of the recommendations of Mr. Hume.'[5] Smith also visited Geneva where he made the acquaintance of Voltaire.

---

3   Meek, **Ignoble**, 127-8
4   Ross, **Smith**, 83
5   Stewart, **Works**, X, 45

The correspondence and conversations with Turgot and Quesnai were to be particularly important in his later thought.

The period in Paris, is described by Rae.

Smith went more into society in the few months he resided in Paris that at any other period of his life. He was a regular guest in almost all the famous literary salons of that time... Our information about his doings is of course meagre, but there is one week in July 1766 in which we happen to have his name mentioned frequently in the course of the correspondence between Hume and his Paris friends regarding a quarrel with Rousseau, and during that week Smith was on the 21st at Mademoiselle l'Espinasse's, on the 25th at Comtesse de Boufflers', and on the 27th at Baron d'Holbach's, where he had some conversation with Turgot. He was a constant visitor at Madame Riccoboni the novelist's. He attended the meetings of the new economist sect in the apartments of Dr. Quesnay, and though the economic dinners of the elder Mirabeau, the 'Friend of Men', were not begun for a year after, he no doubt visited the Marquis, as we know he visited other members of the fraternity. He went to Compiegne when the Court removed to Compiegne, made frequent excursions to interesting places within reach, and is always seen with troops of friends about him.[1]

It is clear that Smith was starting to develop the ideas in his **Lectures on Jurisprudence** into a book when he was in France.

*The Abbé [Morellet] was a metaphysician as well as an economist, but, according to his account of his conversations with Smith, they seem to have discussed mainly economic subjects – 'the theory of commerce,' he says, 'banking, public credit, and various points in the great work which Smith was then meditating,' i.e. the **Wealth of Nations**. This book had therefore by that time taken shape so far that the author made his Paris friends aware of his occupations upon it, and discussed with them definite points in the scheme of doctrine he was unfolding.*[2]

---

1 Rae, **Smith**, 197
2 Rae, **Smith**, 201

Yet it was not just his conversations in Paris that were important. The time in Toulouse may have been equally important and his recent biographer Ross describes how

> It can be argued, however, that for Smith residence in Toulouse yielded an important stock of facts, additional to those collected in Glasgow, about the economic issues that had seized his imagination. These included the division of labour, extent and fluctuation of market, agricultural and commercial systems, the role of transportation in creating wealth, and the struggle for natural liberty in the economic domain. Thus, a walk from the older part of the city to the **quartier parlementaire** to the south provided a lesson in economic history.[3]

After returning to England in 1766 Smith was until early in 1767 an advisor to Charles Townsend, then chancellor of the exchequer, who was preparing his fatal proposal for taxing the American colonies. It is not difficult to see how that experience coloured much of Smith's later writing on taxation. More generally, his spell outside the University was undoubtedly beneficial. The likely effects are summarized by Stewart.

> He had hitherto lived chiefly within the walls of a University, and although to a mind like his, the observation of human nature on the smallest scale is sufficient to convey a tolerably just conception of what passes on the great theatre of the world, yet it is not to be doubted that the variety of scenes through which he afterwards passed, must have enriched his mind with many new ideas, and corrected many of those misapprehensions of life and manners which the best descriptions of them can scarcely fail to convey.[4]

He returned to Kirkcaldy in May 1767. He had a large stock of data, and a number of theories which he had developed in his lectures. His breadth of reading and personal experience was not limited to Europe. The Americas were of great interest

---

3   Ross, **Smith**, 203
4   Stewart, **Works**, X, 43

to the Glasgow merchants, but Asia and Africa were also now increasingly attractive. From Montesquieu he had learnt that no theory of how the modern world was developing could omit a consideration of East Asia and particularly China, about which a great deal was being learnt, especially in France. But how to synthesize this immense inflow of rich data and theory?

He thought and wrote for six years and then went to London in April 1773 where he spent another two and a half years revising his manuscript. As Rae states, 'Much of the book as we know it must have been written in London.'[1] He had thought when he arrived in London that the book was almost completed,

> *But the researches the author now made in London must have been much more important than he expected, and have occasioned extensive alterations and additions, so that Hume, in congratulating him on the eventual appearance of the work in 1776, wrote, 'It is probably much improved by your last abode in London.' Whole chapters seem to have been put through the forge afresh; and on some of them the author has tool-marked the date of his handiwork himself.*[2]

In particular much of the material on America and the colonial experience was added at this stage. As Rae puts it, '"We may go further and say that the American Colonies constitute the experimental evidence of the essential truth of the book, without which many of its leading positions had been little more than theory." It ought of course to be borne in mind that Smith had been in the constant habit of hearing much about the American Colonies and their affairs during his thirteen years in Glasgow from the intelligent merchants and returned planters of that city.'[3]

---

1 Rae, **Smith**, 264

2 Rae, **Smith**, 264

3 Rae, **Smith**, 265-6

In order to understand the changing world around him, Smith refined a number of the theoretical methods which Montesquieu, David Hume and others were advocating. It is arguable that Smith self-consciously set out to apply the Newtonian method to society and history and that he did this with a more than average understanding of what that method was. One part of his debt lay in his use of mechanical analogies in his analysis, which allowed him to investigate the whole of the emerging capitalist and commercial economy and society as if it were some immensely complex mechanism.

Smith used the metaphor of a machine in most of the branches of his analysis. In his early work on the origin of human languages he had likened their structure and progress to that of machines. 'Smith turns to the machine, as he often does seeking explanatory help when describing systems, to provide an analogy for the "progress of language". Original languages have the vast complexity of primitive machines, and both become simpler when gradually the "different parts are more connected and supplied by one another."'[4] Likewise, he applied the idea in relation to the development of scientific or artistic systems or paradigms.

> *Systems in many respects resemble machines. A machine is a little system, created to perform, as well as to connect together, in reality, those different movements and effects which the artist has occasion for. A system is an imaginary machine invented to connect together in the fancy those different movements and effects which are already in reality performed.*[5]

---

4 Ross, **Smith**, 90
5 Smith, **Philosophical**, 66

Or again, society as a whole could be considered as a vast machine. 'Human society, when we contemplate it in a certain abstract and philosophical light, appears like a great, an immense machine, whose regular and harmonious movements produce a thousand agreeable effects.'[1] Finally, the economy could be regarded as a vast machine. He would have been helped in seeing this by the French physiocrats.[2] The analogy gave him confidence that he was investigating an infinitely complex set of inter-relations, a structure of some sort. Behind the visible world there lay a set of moving parts, obeying certain rules and principles. This had given Newton his inspiration and Smith's critics explicitly saw Smith as attempting to discover the 'laws of motion', not of the physical, but of the social and intellectual universe. It was an analytical system which, as Governor Pownall described it, was 'an institute of the Principia **of those laws of motion**, by which the operations of the community are directed and regulated, and by which they should be examined.'[3]

Above all, it replaced God by an invisible hand, the ghost in the machine, to use Koestler's phrase. It incorporated the important idea of the law of unintended consequences into a philosophy which would provide an underpinning for the new world. Meek captures some of this function when he writes that

> *the notion that **historical** processes were autonomous but law-governed led to (or was closely associated with) the notion that economic processes in a commercial society possessed the same characteristics. The economic 'machine', it was postulated, like the historical 'machine', worked unconsciously but in an orderly and predictable manner to produce results which could be said to be 'subject to law' and which therefore*

---

1 Smith, **Moral**, 463-4
2 See Ross, **Smith**, 216
3 Quoted in Campbell and Skinner, **Smith**, 171

*constituted a perfectly proper field of enquiry for the social scientist...
The historical machine automatically produced 'progress', which was
proclaimed to be (up to a point) a good thing; the economic machine
automatically maximised the rate of growth of the national product,
which was also proclaimed to be (up to a point) a good thing.*[4]

Thus the fact that social, linguistic and economic systems were all like machines, which humans constructed and improved, made them analysable and guaranteed their 'progress'. And all this happened not through design, but by accident, through unintended consequences. If the world was like a machine, the individuals in it were cogs who, unbeknown to them, were playing an important part in its progress. Thus

men in pursuing their own objectives seemed frequently to contribute to outcomes which they did not intend or foresee. This doctrine is sometimes described as the law of 'unintended social outcomes' but is more usually cited, in Smith's case, as the doctrine of the 'invisible hand' - as in the statement that man is 'led by an invisible hand to promote and end which was no part of his intention.'[5]

Yet even with this confidence that the goal was to work out the laws of motion of an immense machine which lay behind language, thought systems, society and economy, Smith was still faced with the daunting task of devising a method of finding out the hidden principles which drove it. Here again he developed an approach which was in the Newtonian tradition. It appears that Smith first encountered Newton's method in his 'third or **magistrand** year at Glasgow', that is in 1739-40, when he was about sixteen. The outline of the course then was: '"[the scholars] are taught two Hours at least by the Professor of **Natural Philosophy**, as that science is improved

---

4 Meek, **Ignoble**, 220-1
5 Campbell and Skinner, **Smith**, 95

by **Sir Isaac Newton**, and attend two Hours in the Week a Course of Experiments. Some continue to attend Lessons of **Mathematicks**, or of the Lessons of the **Laws of Nature and Nations**, or of **Greek**, or **Latin**. (Chamberlayne, 1737: II.iii.13).'"[1]

When Smith returned from Oxford he would have had available the outline of that system published by the recent Professor of Mathematics at Edinburgh, Colin Maclaurin. In his **Account of Sir Isaac Newton's Philosophical Discoveries** (1748) Maclaurin noted that the scientist

> *should begin with phenomena, or effects, and from them investigate the powers or causes that operate in nature; that from particular causes we should proceed to the more general ones, till the argument ends in the most general: this is the method of **analysis**. Being once possessed of these causes, we should then descend in a contrary order, and from them, as established principles, explain all the phenomena that are their consequences, and prove our explications; and this is the synthesis. It is evident that, as in mathematics, so in natural philosophy, the investigation of difficult things by the method of **analysis**, ought ever to precede the method of composition, or the **synthesis**. For in any other way we can never be sure that we assume the principles that really obtain in nature; and that our system, after we have composed it with great labour, is not mere dream and illusion.*[2]

In other words there was a backwards and forwards between induction and deduction.

The method required a huge amount of data, for if one were to examine the laws of motion behind the 'great machine' of the world, a wide sweep of materials across time and space were needed, as Montesquieu, whose aims were very similar, had found. As regards space, it was important to consider all kinds of civilization at every level. Thus Smith used his experiences

---

1   Ross, **Smith**, 55
2   Quoted in Campbell and Skinner, **Smith**, 92

in France, Glasgow and elsewhere, and his collection of travel literature, to learn about China, India, the American Indians and anything else that he could. The work of Du Halde on China, and of Lafitau and others on America were especially important and like Montesquieu he tried to absorb the great rush of new knowledge pouring into Europe into his general theories. He was able to do this the more effectively because, like Montaigne, Smith maintained a lofty and detached relativism. For example, he recognized that in aesthetics, as well as in everything else, standards were variable and there was nothing that was ultimately 'right'.

> *What different ideas are formed in different nations concerning the beauty of the human shape and countenance! A fair complexion is a shocking deformity upon the coast of Guinea. Thick lips and a flat nose are a beauty. In some nations long ears that hang down upon the shoulders are the objects of universal admiration. In China, if a lady's foot is so large as to be fit to walk upon, she is regarded as a monster of ugliness.*³

He noted that each culture tended to condemn the others as bizarre, without examining their own equally strange practices. Referring to a North American Indian practice of shaping the head into a square form by tying boards round children's heads, he wrote that 'Europeans are astonished at the absurd barbarity of this practice, to which some missionaries have imputed the singular stupidity of those nations among whom it prevails. But when they condemn those savages, they do not reflect that the ladies in Europe had, till within these few years, been endeavouring for near a century past to squeeze the beautiful roundness of their natural shape into a square form of the same kind.'⁴

---

3   Smith, **Moral**, 288
4   Smith, **Moral**, 288

All this comparative data helped him to fill out the general theory of the evolution of human civilizations which was his life's central work, but even the wealth of material left huge gaps. In particular, it was very difficult to know what had happened in periods before written records survived or in oral cultures. To overcome this problem he developed a method which Dugald Stewart termed 'theoretical or conjectural history'. This was history where in the absence of direct evidence, as Stewart put it, '"we are under a necessity of supplying the place of fact by conjecture; and when we are unable to ascertain how men have actually conducted themselves upon particular occasions, of considering in what manner they are likely to have proceeded, from the principles of their nature and the circumstances of their external situation."'[1] Campbell and Skinner point out that 'Smith provided early evidence of the technique, opening his treatment of the development of language by supposing two "savages, who had never been taught to speak, but had been bred up remote from the societies of men."'[2] The method was very close to the Newtonian method. On the basis of the actual evidence one would build up a set of hypotheses or conjectures, moving from the known to the unknown, and then see if these then elicited any further information which refuted or confirmed the 'conjectures'.

One of Smith's most famous instances of 'conjectural history' or model building was his elaboration of the four-stage theory of civilization which has provided the foundation for all of the social sciences since he wrote. Basically Smith divided the

---

1   Campbell and Skinner, **Smith**, 67, quoting Stewart.
2   Campbell and Skinner, **Smith**, 67

history of civilization into the four 'stages' of hunter-gatherer, pastoralist, settled agriculturalist and 'commercial' society. These stages were defined by the mode of gaining a living and were associated with many other features - the density of population, the development of government, the rise of private property, the development of arts and crafts.[3] Through detailed analysis, Ronald Meek has traced this framework back to Smith's lectures of 1751. This was the very year in which Turgot developed a similar theory, and both of them had been inspired by Montesquieu. Meek believes however that Smith took the idea much further than Montesquieu by seeing the stages as naturally developing out of each other, and as primarily determined by the mode of subsistence or earning a living.[4]

Meek is puzzled, however, as to why Smith and Turgot should both seize on a passage in Book XVIII of the **Spirit of the Laws** and simultaneously 'proceed to dynamize it (as it were) and transform it into a new theory of socio-economic development?'[5] It is a puzzle which Meek never really solves, but which we can perhaps resolve by two arguments. Firstly, if we examine Montesquieu more closely, we see that the gap between his theory and Smith's is far less than that assumed by many Smithian scholars. Montesquieu already had a dynamic theory of social change, as in his work on the fall of Rome or the history of feudal Europe. Smith only needed to elaborate a framework that already almost fully existed. Secondly, the feeling of dynamism and 'progress' which we find more pronounced in Smith probably largely reflects his life's experiences. In Montesquieu's home area around Bordeaux and in France in general there was only slight 'progress', if any. The great contrast

---

3 Smith, **Jurisprudence**, 201ff
4 Meek, **Smith**, 29
5 Meek, **Smith**, 29; cf Meek, **Ignoble Savage**, 35

was with England, but that is far less impressive than seeing one's own home area transforming itself within twenty years.

As we have seen, this is exactly what Smith observed in the Glasgow region. He felt the massive and rapid shift between stages two and three as the 'pastoral' stage in the Highlands gave way within a couple of decades to the settled agricultural stage with the aftermath of the battle of Culloden in 1745. And he could observe from his windows and talk to the people who were rapidly bringing about a commercial society and laying the groundwork for an industrial one. It is not surprising that his framework should be more 'dynamic' as he watched two of the four great transformations occurring before his eyes.

The importance of this stadial framework was immense. It was the foundation for Smith's thought and that of Ferguson, Millar, Kames and others. It was elaborated and developed by the those who re-founded the social sciences in the second half of the nineteenth century, strengthened and made into a unified picture of man and nature through the Darwinian vision. It helped provide the framework for the understanding of world history and in particular the mass of new knowledge generated by the expansion of Europe.

We see from this account of Smith's life and method that he was well placed to investigate the riddle of the birth of the modern world. He lived at its edge, on the border of English civilization, but he also lived at its epicentre, the same corridor where James Watt was revolutionizing the design of the steam engine and hence providing the mechanism to unlock the power to sustain the industrial revolution. Smith was also a part of a great tradition and network of thinkers, from the Greek philosophers onwards.

Although we tend to think of great thinkers as isolated geniuses, of course their views are largely shaped by a complex network of other minds. In many ways, therefore, what we call 'Adam Smith' is a composite, a concentration into one life of numerous trains of thought. Smith synthesized and organized them, but it is no detraction from his greatness to realize that he was just part of a great river through which much of western speculation flowed. Smith undoubtedly owed a heavy debt to the French physiocrats.[1] He owed a good deal to Sir James Steuart.[2] He interests were close to those of Henry Home, Lord Kames, and he said that '"we must every one of us acknowledge Kames for our master".[3] His work overlapped with that of Josiah Tucker.[4] Through his teacher Frances Hutcheson he learnt from the Dutch jurists.

Above all he owed a debt to Hutcheson himself. Five days a week, when he was in his mid-teens studying for his M.A. in Glasgow, he would attend the inspiring 'perfection' of Hutcheson, covering jurisprudence and politics. Leechman in 1755 described Hutcheson's 'civic humanist theme of the importance of civil and religious liberty for human happiness.'[5] Leechman wrote that

> *as a warm love of liberty, and manly zeal for promoting it, were ruling principles in his own breast, he always insisted upon it at great length, and with the greatest strength of argument and earnestness of persuasion: and he had such success on this important point, that few, if any, of his pupils, whatever contrary prejudices they might bring along with them, ever left him without favourable notions of that side of the question which he espoused and defended.*[6]

---

1   Skinner, **System**, 123ff
2   See Skinner in Jones and Skinner, **Adam Smith Reviewed**, ch.10
3   Quoted in Stocking, 'Scotland', 66; see the whole article for an outline of Kames' thought
4   See the interesting summary of the relations by Stern in his introduction to **Josiah Tucker**.
5   Ross, **Smith**, 54
6   Leechman, 1755 quoted in Ross, **Smith**, 54

Smith's work was also connected to that of our other major thinkers, all of whom helped compose the puzzle for him and provided their own answers from which he drew. From Montesquieu's work Smith derived part of his central methodology, in particular the idea of tracing the development of certain institutional forms through a series of stages. Smith was also encouraged to undertake comparative speculation by the **Spirit of the Laws**.

A second influence was the poet Alexander Pope, whose **Essay on Man** summarized many of the contradictions between wealth and morality which would lie at the centre of Smith's analysis. The battle between 'self-love' or selfishness and social virtues, constituting the central tension in the emerging capitalist world which Smith would dissect, is Pope's theme, and his resolution of the conflict is almost identical to that proposed by Smith. Pope considers the essence of individualistic capitalism and the way it transmutes selfish competition into public wealth.

Both Pope and Smith were influenced by the philosopher Bolingbroke, to whom Pope dedicated the **Essay on Man**. Pope also puts into verse some of the key constituents of Smith's famous theory of the 'invisible hand', that is of the orderliness and fixed laws which lie behind the apparently chaotic flux of events. Many of these themes are also echoed in the work of another writer who influenced Smith, Bernard Mandeville.

Mandeville invented the phrase 'the division of labour' and analyzed the mechanism in a way that was helpful to Smith. A second overlap was in Mandeville's famous posing of the paradox of 'private vice, public benefit'. Finally, Mandeville argued forcefully for minimal government interference or laissez-faire, an idea which Smith explored in greater detail.[1]

---

1 See Mandeville, **Fable of the Bees**

The final influence to be considered was the largest of all, namely that of Smith's closest intellectual friend, the slightly older philosopher David Hume. They shared many views, for instance on trade, taxation and population growth. One area where Hume tried to resolve a central problem which also lies at the heart of Smith's endeavour was how the production of wealth had grown in Europe despite the strong tendency towards predation on wealth.

Hume elegantly outlined the problem, the normal tendency to use any growth in wealth or technology to increase centralized power and social inequality, which in turn would crush further development. Furthermore, he provided an ingenious set of arguments to explain how, once only, the trap had been avoided. He praised manufacture and commerce and explained not only its economic, but also its social and political benefits. He showed how a market economy could become self-sustaining and why international trade benefited everyone. He described the virtuous circle by which increased wealth might lead to a balance of power and to individual liberty, which would in turn lead to further wealth. He showed how a prosperous middle class was central to this process.

Hume's wide-ranging mind also contemplated Montesquieu's question of why Europe seemed to be economically dynamic, while China seemed to be 'stationary', and he put forward several ingenious suggestions which overlap with those which Smith was to develop. He traced the chain of causes from ecology to economy and described the advantages of the political and cultural pluralism of Europe. He showed how such pluralism allowed technological growth and how competition led to wealth accumulation, documenting the advantages of a set of independent units placed within a loosely united civilization. Finally, he explored the question of why England had been more successful than any other country in linking social, religious and political independence to the creation of wealth.[1]

Many of these insights were incorporated into Smith's work through a process of discussion and correspondence, and through reading Hume's essays. Yet as with all the thinkers whom Smith encountered, he transmuted and recast their arguments into a new and compelling synthesis which is his own. Given Smith's enormous concentration, deep knowledge and stimulating contacts, we may wonder what his answer was to the riddle of the origins, nature and causes of the central features of a newly emerging world.

---

[1] See Macfarlane, 'David Hume'

TWO

Growth and Stasis

ADAM SMITH'S ECONOMICS were based on a broad philosophical tradition concerned with natural law and human nature. The basic premise here, which he derived from Pope, Hutcheson and others, was that man and the natural laws of the universe were in tune. The secret was to release the inhibitions and constraints and then there would be development.

Smith's apparent belief in the natural tendency towards progress, and particularly economic progress, is well known. There was the early statement that 'Little else is requisite to carry a State to the highest degree of opulence from the lowest barbarism, but peace, easy taxes, and a tolerable administration of justice; all the rest being brought about by the natural course of things.'[2] Dugald Stewart believed that in his **Wealth of Nations**, Smith had given a 'theoretical delineation' of the 'natural progress of opulence in a country' and the causes, 'which have inverted this order in the different countries of modern Europe.'[3] Furthermore Stewart elaborated what he saw to be Smith's aim, which was to bring human institutions into line with the 'nature of things', which would then lead to the natural growth of wealth. As Stewart saw it,

> the great and leading object of his speculations is, to illustrate the provision made by nature in the principles of the human mind, and

---

2 Stewart, **Works**, X, 68.
3 Stewart, **Works**, X, 36.

> *in the circumstances of man's external situation, for a gradual and progressive augmentation in the means of national wealth; and to demonstrate, that the most effectual plan for advancing a people to greatness, is to maintain that order of things which nature has pointed out, by allowing every man, as long as he observes the rules of justice, to pursue his own interest in his own way, and to bring both his industry and his capital into the freest competition with those of his fellow-citizens.[1]*

This attempt to free the natural instincts of man is behind Smith's famous description of man's competitive and rational drives. Smith assumes that the force which leads to the division of labour and accumulation of wealth is 'a certain propensity in human nature...to truck, barter, and exchange one thing for another'. This is a distinctive and original feature of mankind, connected to the development of reason and speech. 'It is common to all men, and to be found in no other race of animals, which seem to know neither this nor any other species of contracts.'[2] One could go back even further;

> *If we should enquire into the principle in the human mind on which this disposition of trucking is founded, it is clearly the natural inclination every one has to persuade. The offering of a shilling, which to us appears to have so plain and simple a meaning, is in reality offering an argument to persuade one to do so and so as it is for his interest. Men always endeavour to persuade others to be of their opinion even when the matter is of no consequence to them.[3]*

Once this natural tendency is allowed freedom, the division of labour will mean that 'Every man thus lives by exchanging, or becomes in some measure a merchant, and the society itself grows to be what is properly a commercial society.'[4]

---

1 Stewart, **Works**, X, 60
2 Smith, **Wealth**, I, 17
3 Smith, **Jurisprudence**, 352.
4 Smith, **Wealth**, I, 26

One of Smith's central concerns was to explain, why, all else being equal, wealth would grow 'naturally'. One part of his argument lay in a theory of the natural creativity and ingenuity of man, very much along the lines of 'necessity is the mother of invention'. He took it as an axiom that it was a special property of man, as distinct from other animals, to be inventive in relation to technology. 'Man has received from the bounty of nature reason and ingenuity, art, contrivan<c>e, and capacity of improvement far superior to that which she has bestowed on any of the other animals, but is at the same time in a much more helpless and destitute condition with regard to the support and comfort of his life.'[5] The push towards invention thus came from the fact that humans were so poorly supplied in their natural state.

He pointed to the fact that nearly all inventions came out of a desire to improve the material world. 'Indeed to supply the wants of **meat**, **drink**, cloathing, and lodging allmost the whole of the arts and sciences have been invented and improved.'[6] He asked 'How many artists are employed to prepare those things with which the shops of the uphorsterrer, the draper, the mercer and cloth-seller <?>, to clip the wool, pick it, sort it, spin, comb, twist, weave, scour, dye, etc. the wool, and a hundred other operators engaged on each different commodities?'[7] This led him to the belief that 'in a certain view of things all the arts, the science<s>, law and government, wisdom, and even virtue itself tend all to this one thing, the providing meat, drink, rayment, and lodging for men, which are commonly reckoned the meanest of employments and fit for the pursuit of none but the lowest and meanest of the people.'[8]

---

5 Smith, **Jurisprudence**, 334
6 Smith, **Jurisprudence**, 337
7 Smith, **Jurisprudence**, 337
8 Smith. **Jurisprudence**, 338

Everything, in the end, came down to practical necessities, to the shifting of atoms. 'Even law and government have these as their finall end and ultimate object. They give the inhabitants of the country liberty and security in the cultivate the land which they possess in safety, and their benign influence gives room and opportunity for the improvement of all the various arts and sciences.'[1] He was deeply aware of the complex chain of operations that had led to the apparently simple material objects around him. 'How many have been required to furnish out the coarse linnen shirt [which] he wears; the tanned and dressed-leather-shoes; his bed which he rest<s> in; the grate at which he dresses his victuals; the coals he burns, which have been brought by a long land sea carriage.'[2]

Yet there was still the puzzle of how all these technologies, however desirable, had emerged. Here Smith seems to have made a distinction between small 'micro' inventions, craft or implicit knowledge and 'macro' or 'scientific' or explicit knowledge. He believed that mankind's ingenuity and the concentrated attention which was one consequence of an increasing division of labour would automatically generate small inventions.

> *When one is employed constantly on one thing his mind will naturally be employed in devising the most proper means of improving it. It was probably a farmer who first invented the plow, tho the plough wright perhaps... And there is none of the inventions of that machine so mysterious that one or other of these could not have been the inventor of it. The drill plow, the most ingenious of any, was the invention of a farmer.*[3]

He believed that the process was still at work in industrial manufacture. 'But if we go into the work house of any manufacturer in the new works at Sheffiel<d>, Manchester,

---

1   Smith, **Jurisprudence**, 338
2   Smith, **Jurisprudence**, 339
3   Smith. **Jurisprudence**, 346

or Birmingham, or even some towns in Scotland, and enquire concerning the machines, they will tell you that such or such an one was invented by some common workman.'[4]

On the other hand he was also aware that the great 'macro' inventions required a large, non-obvious, leap of imagination. They required 'science' or formalized knowledge of some kind. He made the distinction, as often, with an example.

> *The wheel wright also, by an effort of thought and after long experien<ce>, might contrive the cog wheel which, turne [n] d by a verticall winch, facilitated the labour exceedingly as it gave the man a superior power over it. But the man who first thought of applying a stream of water and still more the blast of the wind to turn this, by an outer wheel in place of a crank, was neither a millar nor a mill-wright but a philosopher, one of those men who, tho they work at nothing themselves, yet by observing all are enabled by this extended way of thinking to apply things together to produce effects to which they seem noway adapted.[5]*

He devoted a good deal of thought to how such 'philosophers' worked and made their discoveries. In essence they had to 'imagine' something that did not yet exist, rather than make minor improvements to what already existed. Their difficulty is summarized as follows, where the process of invention and subsequent refinement is well put.

> *The machines that are first invented to perform any particular movement are always the most complex, and succeeding artists generally discover that, with fewer wheels, with fewer principles of motion, than had originally been employed, the same effects may be more easily produced. The first systems, in the same manner, are always the most complex, and a particular connecting chain, or principle, is generally thought necessary to unite every two seemingly disjointed appearances...[6]*

---

4 Smith, **Jurisprudence**, 351
5 Smith. **Jurisprudence**, 346-7
6 Smith, **Philosophical**, 66

Smith believed that humans were naturally curious and ingenious. If these traits were encouraged, there would be rapid technical progress to improve material well-being. More difficult to explain were the 'macro' inventions, where he would no doubt have stressed the need for money, a network of contacts, leisure and curiosity. He also stressed an 'open' intellectual climate, that is a diversity of religious and political opinions, none of them dominant - a competitive world similar to the free trade and competition of the market. 'One thing that has contributed to the increase of curiosity is that there are now severall sects in Religion and politicall disputes which are greatly dependent on the truth of certain facts.'[1] He had found such a world stimulating in eighteenth-century Scotland.

Smith introduced his principle of the division of labour into his lectures sometime in the 1750s. By the time of his lectures on Jurisprudence in 1766, he was already using his favourite example, the pin-maker.[2] But he also gave other examples where the division of labour had been in operation. For example, if one took a simple iron tool, 'how many hands has it gone thro. The miner, the quarrier, the breaker, the smelter, the forger, the maker of the charcoall to smelt it, the smith, etc. have had a hand in the forming it.'[3] This division of labour was the key to improvement and growing opulence. As Smith put it 'It is the great multiplication of the productions of all the different arts, in consequence of the division of labour, which occasions, in a well-governed society, that universal opulence which extends

---

1 Smith, **Rhetoric**, 102
2 Smith, **Jurisprudence**, 341
3 Smith, **Jurisprudence**, 339

itself to the lowest ranks of the people.'[4] Generalizing from his pin makers, he found that

> *In every other art and manufacture, the effects of the division of labour are similar to what they are in this very trifling one; though, in many of them, the labour can neither be so much subdivided, nor reduced to so great a simplicity of operation. The division of labour, however, so far as it can be introduced, occasions, in every art, a proportionable increase of the productive powers of labour. The separation of different trades and employments from one another, seems to have taken place, in consequence of this advantage. This separation too is generally carried furthest in those countries which enjoy the highest degree of industry and improvement; what is the work of one man in a rude state of society, being generally that of several in an improved one.*[5]

> *The reasons for the increase in production and hence wealth were three-fold. 'This great increase of the quantity of work which, in consequence of the division of labour, the same number of people are capable of performing, is owing to three different circumstances; first to the increase of dexterity in every particular workman; secondly, to the saving of the time which is commonly lost in passing from one species of work to another; and lastly, to the invention of a great number of machines which facilitate and abridge labour, and enable one man to do the work of many.*[6]

For, as he had put it more succinctly in a lecture twelve years earlier, 'the division of labour increases the work performed from three causes: dexterity acquired by doing one simple thing, the saving of time, and the invention of machines which is occasioned by it.'[7] It is interesting that the third of his reasons was rather different. By breaking up a task into its component parts, it could more clearly be seen where a machine could replace a human being.

---

4 Smith, **Wealth**, I, 15

5 Smith, **Wealth**, I, 9

6 Smith, **Wealth**, I, 11

7 Smith, **Jurisprudence**, 350

The advantages in terms of the improvements in technology, including machinery, were equally important, for the division of labour tended to make micro-inventions more likely. A nice example of how this worked, and to prove his point that most mechanical inventions were made by the workers themselves, was as follows. He described how in the first steam engine,

> *a boy was constantly employed to open and shut alternately the communication between the boiler and the cylinder, according as the piston either ascended or descended. One of those boys, who loved to play with his companions, observed that, by tying a string from the handle of the valve which opened this communication to another part of the machine, the valve would open and shut without his assistance, and leave him at liberty to divert himself with his play fellows. One of the greatest improvements that has been made upon this machine, since it was first invented, was in this manner the discovery of a boy who wanted to save his own labour.*[1]

Of course, not only is the story, as the footnote to this passage shows, mythical, but Smith omits the fact that in most societies the boy would have put himself out of a job in this way. Yet the more general point concerning the inter-actions between mechanization and the division of labour is an interesting one. Basically Smith had located the organizational and mechanical side of the industrial revolution. He only lacked the realization of the power of the 'fire engine' as he called it, in other words the steam engine.

He came very close to understanding the potential of new machinery in his early lectures when he discussed the effects of mechanical inventions, and in particular the replacement of human energy by animal, wind and water power.

> *The invention of machines vastly increases the quantity of work which is done. This is evident in the most simple operations. A plow with 2*

---

1   Smith, **Wealth**, I, 13-14

> men and three horses will till more ground than twenty men could dig with the spade. A wind or water mill directed by the miller will do more work than 8 men with hand-mills, and this too with great ease, whereas the handmill was reckoned the hardest labour a man could be put to, and therefore none were employed in it but those who had been guilty of some capitall crime. But the handmill was far from being a contemptible machine, and had required a good deal of ingenuity in the invention.2

Even with James Watt down the corridor, however, he did not realize the revolution that was just emerging as fossil fuels opened up a vast store of carbon energy.

He did, however, notice a further effect of the division of labour beyond improving production and the chances of mechanical inventions. This was that it led to trade and exchange.

> When the division of labour has been once thoroughly established, it is but a very small part of a man's wants which the produce of his own labour can supply. He supplies the far greater part of them by exchanging that surplus part of the produce of his own labour, which is over and above his own consumption, for such parts of the produce of other men's labour as he has occasion for.3

The process was in fact circular and cumulative. Surpluses created exchange or commerce, commerce then encouraged further division of labour and specialization. 'Hence as commerce becomes more and more extensive the division of labour becomes more and more perfect.'4 He could see this, for instance within commerce itself if he compared even the fairly advanced parts of Scotland with London 'A merchant in Glasgow or Aberdeen who deals in linnen will have in his warehouse Irish, Scots, and Hamburgh linnens, but at

---

2 Smith, **Jurisprudence**, 346.
3 Smith, **Wealth**, I, 26
4 Smith, **Jurisprudence**, 356

London there are separate dealers in each of these.'¹ Thus the growth of commercial wealth and division of labour were in many ways two sides of a coin. His dynamic central force was factory production. He had thus almost seen the way in which a commercial economy would break into an industrial one but without the energy revolution could not quite solve the riddle.

❊❊❊

Smith believed that an increase in commercial activity would lead to an improvement in 'civility'. His prime evidence for its moral effects came from a comparison of various European countries.

> *Whenever commerce is introduced into any country, probity and punctuality always accompany it. These virtues in a rude and barbarous country are almost unknown. Of all the nations in Europe, the Dutch, the most commercial, are the most faithfull to their word. The English are more so than the Scotch, but much inferiour to the Dutch, and in the remote parts of this country they <are> far less so than in the commercial parts of it.²*

He believed that this had nothing to do with race, but rather that self-interest motivated it.

> *There is no natural reason why an Englishman or Scotchman should not be as punctual in performing agreements as a Dutchman. It is far more reduceable to self interest, that general principle which regulates the actions of every man, and which leads men to act in a certain manner from views of advantage, and is as deeply implanted in an Englishman as a Dutchman. A dealer is afraid of losing his character, and is scrupulous in observing every engagement.³*

---

1   Smith, **Jurisprudence**, 355
2   Smith, **Jurisprudence**, 538
3   .Smith, **Jurisprudence**, 538

The reason why the balance shifted from competitive individualism to co-operative behaviour lay in the frequency of transactions. 'Wherever dealings are frequent, a man does not expect to gain so much by any one contract as by probity and punctuality in the whole, and a prudent dealer, who is sensible of his real interest, would rather chuse to lose what he has a right to than give any ground for suspicion.'[4] Thus honesty became the best policy. Reputation in the longer term was more important than short-term gain.

Smith was also interested in the effects of commerce on art and aesthetics. He started by noting that there was a shift in literary style, from poetry and allusive, dramatic, art, to the more practical prose. 'Prose is naturally the Language of Business; as Poetry is of pleasure and amusement. Prose is the Stile in which all the common affairs of Life all Business and Agreements are made.'[5] But he then widened this out to improvements in all arts. 'Tis the Introduction of Commerce or at lest of opulence which is commonly the attendent of Commerce which first brings on the improvement of Prose. Opulence and Commerce commonly precede the improvement of arts, and refinement of every Sort.'[6] He may have had in mind that much art requires leisure, patronage and so on, but there is an implication of something more when he talks of 'refinement'. The mentality bred by commercial societies took them away from the 'rough' manners of warrior societies. He may have had the contrast of the Highland lairds of his youth and contemporary Edinburgh or Glasgow in his mind.

Like most great thinkers, Smith's thought arose out of and reflected a series of contradictions. One of these was

---

4   Smith, **Jurisprudence**, 539
5   Smith, **Rhetoric**, 137
6   Smith, **Rhetoric**, 137

between his belief that, all else being equal, there was a natural tendency towards the increase of wealth and his realization that in fact such progress only fitfully occurred.[1] This was linked to a second contradiction. Even those countries which seemed to have progressed farthest seemed to have hit some kind of ceiling. In trying to solve these problems he laid the foundations of economics.

Smith did not find it difficult to see why, despite the 'tendency' towards opulence, many societies and civilizations had, in their early stages, remained poor for so long. There was a vicious circle of poverty 'Bare subsistence is almost all that a savage can procure, and having no stock to begin upon, nothing to maintain him but what is produced by the exertion of his own strength, it is no wonder that he continues long in an indigent state.'[2] Invoking the division of labour, he wrote 'This is one great cause of the slow progress of opulence in every country; till some stock be produced there can be no division of labour, and before a division of labour take place there can be very little accumulation of stock.'[3] People were forced to share any surplus rather than accumulate a reasonable capital. 'The other arts were all proportionally uncultivated. In was impossible for a man in this state, then, to lay out his whole fortune on himself; the only way his had to dispose of it was to give it out to others.'[4] The ecology was often unimproved and inhospitable; '...Tartary and Araby labour under both these difficulties. For in the first place their soil is very poor and such as will hardly admit of culture of any sort, the one on account of its dryness and hardness, the other on account of

---

1 Cf. Meek, **Ignoble**, 238-9 who notes that Smith was setting up a 'tendency' which was very often not fulfilled.
2 Smith, **Jurisprudence**, 521
3 Smith, **Jurisprudence**, 522
4 Smith, **Jurisprudence**, 50

its steep and uneven surface.'⁵ Communications were often very poor - particularly with an absence of water transport. 'This is still the case in Asia and other eastern countries; all inland commerce is carried on by great caravans, consisting of several thousands, for mutual defence, with wagons, etca.'⁶

Hovering over all this was constant predation. There was internal predation of the powerful on the weak. 'There could be little accumulation of stock, because the indolent, which would be the greatest number, would live upon the industrious, and spend whatever they produced.'⁷ Even if such internal predation could be controlled, there was the danger from foreign invaders. 'Among neighbouring nations in a barbarous state there are perpetual wars, one continualy invading and plundering the other, and tho' private property be secured from the violence of neighburs, it is in danger from hostile invasions. In this manner it is next to impossible that any accumulation of stock can be made.'⁸ He pointed out that 'When people find themselves every moment in danger of being robbed of all they possess, they have no motive to be industrious.'⁹ He concluded that 'Thus large tracts of country are often laid waste and all the effects carried away: Germany too was in the same condition about the fall of the Roman Empire. Nothing can be more an obstacle to the progress of opulence.'¹⁰ Nevertheless great civilizations had arisen and overcome these difficulties. Smith's pondered about what traps or impediments then lay in their path. Why was the 'tendency' often so weak and ineffective?

---

5   Smith, **Jurisprudence**, 223
6   Smith, **Jurisprudence**, 528
7   Smith, **Jurisprudence**, 522
8   Smith, **Jurisprudence**, 522
9   Smith, **Jurisprudence**, 522
10 Smith, **Jurisprudence**, 522

Smith's travels on the Continent, his reading of history and accounts of parts of Asia, led him to a number of conclusions. One was that economic development was possible and indeed had occurred in many parts of Europe. One example of this was his own experience in the rapidly expanding economy of lowland Scotland, which was widened when he was able to make an interesting three-way comparison between England, France and Scotland.

> *When you go from Scotland to England, the difference which you may remark between the dress and countenance of the common people in the one country and in the other, sufficiently indicates the difference in their condition. The contrast is still greater when you return from France. France, though no doubt a richer country than Scotland, seems not to be going forward so fast. It is a common and even a popular opinion in the country, that it is going backwards...[1]*

Even though he thought this opinion 'ill founded' he was aware of a check there.

The concept of 'going backwards' is an interesting one and France is one of his prime examples of a slowing down, if not retreat. While in England the payments for labour had been rising for some time,

> *In France, a country not altogether so prosperous, the money price of labour has, since the middle of the last century, been observed to sink gradually with the average money price of corn. Both in the last century and in the present, the day-wages of common labour are there said to have been pretty uniformly about the twentieth part of the average price of the septier of wheat, a measure which contains a little more than four Winchester bushels. In Great Britain the real recompense of labour, it has already been shown, the real quantities of the necessaries and conveniences of life which are given to the labourer, has increased considerably during the course of the present century. The rise in its*

---

1 Smith, **Wealth**, I, 102

> *money price seems to have been the effect, not of any diminution of the value of silver in the general market of Europe, but of a rise in the real price of labour in the particular market of Great Britain, owing to the peculiarly happy circumstances of the country.*[2]

Smith was interested in both the cross-sectional wealth of a nation and changes over time - the dynamics of the situation. All of Europe had seen a sudden spurt forward after about 1500, though certain countries had faltered and even 'gone backwards' later. Particularly striking was the shift of gravity from the Mediterranean to the northern countries.

> *Since the discovery of America, the greater part of Europe has been much improved. England, Holland, France, and Germany; even Sweden, Denmark, and Russia, have all advanced considerably both in agriculture and in manufactures. Italy seems not to have gone backwards. The fall of Italy preceded the conquest of Peru. Since that time it seems rather to have recovered a little. Spain and Portugal, indeed, are supposed to have gone backwards. Portugal, however, is but a very small part of Europe, and the declension of Spain is not, perhaps, so great as is commonly imagined.*[3]

Thus Italy was more or less stationery, Portugal and Spain declining.

The northern countries had been increasing in wealth but had reached an equilibrium. France had expanded but by the mid eighteenth century seemed more or less stationary. Holland, 'in proportion to the extent of the land and the number of its inhabitants' was 'by far the richest country in Europe.'[4] It was 'in proportion to the extent of its territory and the number of its people' a 'richer country than England'. The 'wages of labour are said to be higher in Holland than in

---

2 Smith, **Wealth**, I, 223
3 Smith, **Wealth**, I, 225
4 Smith, **Wealth**, I, 395

England and the Dutch, it is well known, trade upon lower profits than any people in Europe.'¹ Yet Holland also seemed to be stuck, even if it might not be true, as some thought, that it was actually declining.

The one country in Europe which seemed still to be growing rapidly was England.

> *Since the time of Henry VIII the wealth and revenue of the country have been continually advancing, and, in the course of their progress, their pace seems rather to have been gradually accelerated than retarded. They seem, not only to have been going on, but to have been going on faster and faster. The wages of labour have been continually increasing during the same period, and in the greater part of the different branches of trade and manufactures the profits of stock have been diminishing.²*

As Smith surveyed its history all he could see was a gradual but accelerating growth in wealth, century by century, since Roman times.

> *The annual produce of the land and labour of England again, was certainly much greater at the restoration [1660], than we can suppose it to have been about an hundred years before, at the accession of Elizabeth [1558]. At this period too, we have all reason to believe, the country was much more advanced in improvement, than it had been about a century before, towards the close of the dissensions between the houses of York and Lancaster. Even then it was, probably, in a better condition than it had been at the Norman conquest, and at the Norman conquest, than during the confusion of the Saxon Heptarchy. Even at this early period, it was certainly a more improved country than at the invasion of Julius Caesar, when its inhabitants were nearly in the same state with the savages in North America.³*

---

1 Smith, **Wealth**, I, 102
2 Smith, **Wealth**, I, 100
3 Smith, **Wealth**, I, 366

However Smith's mind ranged beyond Europe. If continued growth was unusual there, how were other areas faring? Here he made a triadic comparison between the New World of North America, the old world of Europe, and the far Eastern world of China. Summing up his impressions of these three, he found that growth was 'rapidly progressive' in North America, 'slow and gradual' in Europe, and 'altogether stationary' in China. The case of the great civilization of China was particularly intriguing and a good negative case to test out his theories.

Basing himself on similar sources to those used by Montesquieu, that is the work of Du Halde and the Jesuit missionaries, Smith described the wealthy but stationary state of China, which he thought had roughly existed for at least the last four hundred years or so.

> *China has been long one of the richest, that is, one of the most fertile, best cultivated, most industrious, and most populous countries in the world. It seems, however, to have been long stationary. Marco Polo, who visited it more than five hundred years ago, describes its cultivation, industry, and populousness, almost in the same terms in which they are described by travellers in the present times. It had perhaps, even long before his time, acquired that full complement of riches which the nature of its laws and institutions permits it to acquire.*[4]

Though it was stationary it did not seem to be declining.

> *China, however, though it may perhaps stand still, does not seem to go backwards. Its towns are no-where deserted by their inhabitants. The lands which had once been cultivated are no-where neglected. The same or very nearly the same annual labour must therefore continue to be performed, and the funds destined for maintaining it must not, consequently, be sensibly diminished.*[5]

---

4 Smith, **Wealth**, I, 80
5 Smith, **Wealth**, I, 81

Thus it had apparently reached a steady state which others could envy.

Yet while China was 'a much richer country than any part of Europe' it was not only 'stationary' but its common people lived in some hardship.

> *The accounts of all travellers, inconsistent in many other respects, agree in the low wages of labour, and in the difficulty which a labourer finds in bringing up a family in China. If by digging the ground a whole day he can get what will purchase a small quantity of rice in the evening, he is contented. The condition of artificers is, if possible, still worse. Instead of waiting indolently in their work-houses, for the calls of their customers, as in Europe, they are continually running about the streets with the tools of their respective trades, offering their service, and as it were begging employment. The poverty of the lower ranks of people in China far surpasses that of the most beggarly nations in Europe.*[1]

There were thus two puzzles. One was why had China remained stationary. The other was, why, in such a rich country, were the lower ranks so miserably poor. Smith suggested that the lack of progress was due to the inward-looking, bounded, nature of China. The other element was the cultivation of rice, which made labour over-abundant and provided large surpluses which encouraged economic inequality.

The bias towards agriculture and against manufacturing and especially foreign trade was noted by Smith.

> *The policy of China favours agriculture more than all other employments. In China, the condition of a labourer is said to be as much superior to that of an artificer; as in most parts of Europe, that of an artificer is to that of a labourer. In China, the great ambition of every man is to get possession of some little bit of land, either in property or in lease; and leases are there said to be granted upon very moderate terms, and to be sufficiently secured to the lessees. The Chinese have little*

---

1 Smith, **Wealth**, I, 80-1

respect for foreign trade. Your beggarly commerce! was the language in which the Mandarins of Peking used to talk to Mr. de Lange, the Russian envoy, concerning it. Except with Japan, the Chinese carry on, themselves, and in their own bottoms, little or no foreign trade; and it is only into one or two ports of their kingdom that they even admit the ships of foreign nations. Foreign trade, therefore, is, in China, every way confined within a much narrower circle than that to which it would naturally extend itself, if more freedom was allowed to it, either in their own ships, or in those of foreign nations.[2]

It was true that China had a very large internal trade.

the great extent of the empire of China, the vast multitude of its inhabitants, the variety of climate, and consequently of production in its different provinces, and the easy communication by means of water carriage between the greater part of them, render the home market of that country of so great extent, as to be alone sufficient to support very great manufactures, and to admit of very considerable subdivisions of labour. The home market of China is, perhaps, in extent, not much inferior to the market of all the different countries of Europe put together.[3]

Yet this enormous internal opportunity had turned the Chinese inwards. Without foreign trade they became too bounded and unable to benefit from external ideas and improvements. The following passage, which echoes to a considerable extent the ideas of Du Halde upon whom Smith was dependent, summarizes one of Smith's main theories to account for China's stagnation, and by implication one of the reasons for Europe's relative dynamism.

A more extensive foreign trade, however, which to this great home market added the foreign market of all the rest of the world; especially if any considerable part of this trade was carried on in Chinese ships; could scarce fail to increase very much the manufactures of China,

---

2 Smith, **Wealth**, II, 201

3 Smith, **Wealth**, II, 202

and to improve very much the productive powers of its manufacturing industry. By a more extensive navigation, the Chinese would naturally learn the art of using and constructing themselves all the different machines made use of in other countries, as well as the other improvements of art and industry which are practised in all the different parts of the world. Upon their present plan they have little opportunity of improving themselves by the example of any other nation; except that of the Japanese.[1]

Another thing Smith noted, like Montesquieu, was that the fruitfulness of rice led to a very dense population. 'In rice countries, which generally yield two, sometimes three crops in the year, each of them more plentiful than any common crop of corn, the abundance of food must be much greater than in any corn country of equal extent. Such countries are accordingly much more populous.'[2]

One consequence was that the rich could purchase large numbers of followers in a way that was impossible in Europe. Wealthy people

having a greater super-abundance of food to dispose of beyond what they themselves can consume, have the means of purchasing a much greater quantity of the labour of other people. The retinue of a grandee in China or Indostan accordingly is, by all accounts, much more numerous and splendid than that of the richest subjects in Europe.[3]

Smith also notes that China and India though not 'much inferior' were definitely 'inferior' in their 'manufacturing art and industry' to Europe.[4] At this point he does not make any connection between the availability of very cheap and plentiful labour and the relative inferiority of manufacturing and machinery.

---

1 Smith, **Wealth**, II, 202
2 Smith, **Wealth**, I, 228
3 Smith, **Wealth**, I, 228
4 Smith, **Wealth**, I, 229

A second consequence of rice cultivation was that it encouraged extreme social stratification, a class of landlords. This was again because of the bountifulness of rice.

> *Though its cultivation, therefore, requires more labour, a much greater surplus remains after maintaining all that labour. In those rice countries, therefore, where rice is the common and favourite vegetable food of the people, and where the cultivators are chiefly maintained with it, a greater share of this greater surplus should belong to the landlord than in corn countries.*[5]

The other effect of the bountifulness of rice is to produce not only a very dense population, but one which will continue to grow ever more dense at every opportunity. In this way, as Smith noted, it tends to have the same effect as potatoes. Because of the much higher food value of potatoes, 'much superior to what is produced by a field of wheat', Smith thought that

> *Should this root ever become in any part of Europe, like rice in some rice countries, the common and favourite vegetable food of the people, so as to occupy the same proportion of the lands in tillage which wheat and other sorts of grain for human food do at present, the same quantity of cultivated land would maintain a much greater number of people, and the labourers being generally fed with potatoes, a greater surplus would remain after replacing all the stock and maintaining all the labour employed in cultivation. A greater share of this surplus too would belong to the landlord. Population would increase, and rents would rise much beyond what they are at present.*[6]

Thus one would simultaneously have richer landlords and a swarming population. The same was true of rice. It encouraged

---

5   Smith, **Wealth**, I, 178
6   Smith, **Wealth**, I, 179

the population to rise. 'Marriage is encouraged in China.'[1] If he had been able to obtain better data he would have realized that since the late seventeenth century Chinese population had risen very fast. What he was roughly describing in his description of a long stationary period is the famous 'high level equilibrium trap'.[2]

We can thus see that Smith had isolated two central problems. The first was, how had certain countries managed to achieve a high level of opulence. The second was, what was the nature of the obstacles or ceilings which Italy, Spain and Portugal had first hit, which seemed to afflict Eastern Europe and particularly Poland, and had even finally halted the wealthiest countries in the world, Holland and China.

Because the causes of growth and the obstacles to growth are usually opposite sides to the same coin, it appears impossible to separate them, so I will try to take them one by one and see how Smith analysed the pair. In proceeding to this analysis it is worth remembering Smith's approach and data. He was juggling with space - China versus Europe versus North America, England versus Scotland versus France versus Holland versus other European countries - and also with time, with the economic history of each of these entities over the last five hundred years or so.

1　Smith, **Wealth**, I, 81
2　Elvin, **Pattern**, 203

THREE

Of Wealth and Liberty

One of the conditions for growth was the development of towns. Adam Smith's experience in Glasgow, where he could see before his eyes the effect of the rapid growth of a city and could talk to prosperous manufacturers and traders, gives his account of the role of towns in economic growth a particular depth and interest. It is also fascinating because it is so deeply ambivalent and contradictory, both laudatory and condemning of this growth.

In a chapter significantly entitled 'Of the Natural Progress of Opulence', he started by pointing out that towns were important to commercial development.

> *The great commerce of every civilized society, is that carried on between the inhabitants of the town and those of the country. It consists in the exchange of rude for manufactured produce, either immediately, or by the intervention of money, or of some sort of paper which represents money. The country supplies the town with the means of subsistence, and the materials of manufacture. The town repays this supply by sending back a part of the manufactured produce to the inhabitants of the country.*[3]

This was welcome for 'The gains of both are mutual and reciprocal, and the division of labour is in this, as in all other cases, advantageous to all the different persons...'[4] Elsewhere he pointed out in a chapter titled 'How the Commerce of the

---

3   Smith, **Wealth**, I, 401
4   Smith, **Wealth**, I, 401

Towns Contributed to the Improvement of the Country' that there were three effects on the countryside. As he put it in the marginal headings these were 'because they afforded (1) a ready market for its produce (2) because merchants bought land in the country and improved it and (3) because order and good government were introduced.'[1]

It is worth quoting Smith a little further. He wrote that

> *commerce and manufactures gradually introduced order and good government, and with them, the liberty and security of individuals, among the inhabitants of the country, who had before lived almost in a continual state of war with their neighbours, and of servile dependency upon their superiors. This, though it has been the least observed, is by far the most important of all their effects. Mr. Hume is the only writer who, so far as I know, has hitherto taken notice of it.*[2]

The bands of retainers were dismissed and the lords became prosperous capitalists.

Smith was fully aware that free trading and manufacturing towns were unlikely to emerge from agrarian civilizations. Foreshadowing Marx and Weber he gives an excellent sketch of their chance emergence and their peculiarity in the West. He describes how after the Fall of the Roman Empire 'Free Burghs' began to emerge in the West, having control over their own taxation and their own government.

> *They were gradually at the same time erected into a commonality or corporation, with the privilege of having magistrates and a town-council of their own, of making bye-laws for their own government, of building walls for their own defence, and of reducing all their inhabitants under a sort of military discipline, by obliging them to watch and ward; that is, as anciently understood, to guard and defend those walls against all attacks and surprises by night as well as by day. In England they were*

---

[1] Smith, **Wealth**, I, 432-3
[2] Smith, **Wealth**, I, 433

generally exempted from suit to the hundred and country courts; and all such pleas as should arise among them, the pleas of the crown excepted, were left to the decision of their own magistrates. In other countries much greater and more extensive jurisdictions were frequently granted to them.[3]

Such a development was amazing. For instance in relation to their ability to tax themselves, it was extraordinary that the sovereigns of all the different countries of Europe

should have exchanged in this manner for a rent certain, never more to be augmented, that branch of the revenue, which was, perhaps, of all others the most likely to be improved by the natural course of things, without either expense or attention of their own: and that they should, besides, have in this manner voluntarily erected a sort of independent republics in the heart of their own dominions.[4]

Given the possibility of predating on this, why were they set free?

Here Smith develops the ingenious theory that basically they managed to escape through the tension between the King and his feudal nobles. His account of this process, whereby the King sided with the towns in his battles with the nobles, is worth giving in full. Starting with the feudal lords, he noted that

the wealth of the burghers never failed to provoke their envy and indignation, and they plundered them upon every occasion without mercy or remorse. The burghers naturally hated and feared the lords. The king hated and feared them too; but though perhaps he might despise, he had no reason either to hate or fear the burghers. Mutual interest, therefore, disposed them to support the king, and the king to support them against the lords. They were the enemies of his enemies, and it was his interest to render them as secure and independent of those enemies as he could. By granting them magistrates of their own,

---

3   Smith, **Wealth**, I, 423

4   Smith, **Wealth**, I, 423

> *the privilege of making bye-laws for their own government, that of building walls for their own defence, and that of reducing all their inhabitants under a sort of military discipline, he gave them all the means of security and independency of the barons which it was in his power to bestow.*[1]

The support of the King built up the strength of those who lived in the towns, forming them into a separate and powerful estate of their own.

> *These burghers were such, and were therefore greatly encouraged by them, and we find accordingly that all the burghers and freed sort of slaves who lived in the villages or towns, which any villain became who left his master and lived in one of these towns for a year without being claimd, had the liberty of marrying whom they pleased, of free trade, etc., without any toll. They were afterwards formed into corporations holding in capite [directly] of the king, having a jurisdiction and territory for which they paid a certain rent.'*[2]

As their power grew, they began to defend themselves against the predations of local lords.

> *In this manner these small towns became free and able to protect themselves, as they had a stout stone wall about the town and kept a constant watch and ward, which was one part of the duty of a burgher, and were always ready for arms and battle to defend themselves against the attempts of the lords, who frequently disturbed them and often plundered their towns.*[3]

The danger, however, was that they would go too far in their independence. If they lost their alliance with the ruler, they might prosper for a time. This was exactly what happened in Italy and Switzerland, where 'on account either of their

---

[1] Smith, **Wealth**, I, 424

[2] Smith, **Jurisprudence**, 256.

[3] Smith, **Jurisprudence**, 256.

distance from the principal seat of government, of the natural strength of the country itself, or of some other reason, the sovereign came to lose the whole of his authority, the cities generally became independent republics, and conquered all the nobility in their neighbourhood; obliging them to pull down their castles in the country, and to live, like other peaceable inhabitants, in the city.'[4] But in the long run they were too small to be viable and were finally crushed by foreign invaders, as in Italy.

In France and England, however, 'the cities had no opportunity of becoming entirely independent.' Yet they jealously preserved some autonomy and, for instance, 'the sovereign could impose no tax upon them...without their own consent.'[5] Thus they emerged as expanding oases of order and rational wealth production in an agrarian landscape otherwise characterized by predatory, feuding, lords. As Smith put it in the marginal heading: 'In consequence of this greater security of the towns industry flourished and stock accumulated there earlier than in the country.' Thus 'Order and good government, and along with them the liberty and security of individuals, were, in this manner, established in cities, at a time when the occupiers of land in the country were exposed to every sort of violence.'[6] Art and good manners also flourished. 'Wherever the Inhabitants of a city are rich and opulent, where they enjoy the necessaries and conveniences of life in ease and Security, there the arts will be cultivated and refinement of manners a neverfailing attendent.'[7]

Thus, as many later commentators would argue, the growth of towns and the growth of commercial capitalism went hand

---

[4] Smith, **Wealth**, I, 425-6
[5] Smith, **Wealth**, I, 426
[6] Smith, **Wealth**, I, 426
[7] Smith, Rhetoric, 137.

in hand, and Smith has given some hints why in the fragmented and balanced politics of Europe a type of 'free town' should emerge which later Weber was to show was entirely different to that in the absolutist Empires of the East.[1]

So what was Smith's objection to towns? He thought, ultimately, that town and countryside would become opposed. He believed, as he put it, that agriculture was primary and trade and town manufacture was secondary.

> *As subsistence is, in the nature of things, prior to convenience and luxury, so the industry which procures the former, must necessarily be prior to that which ministers to the latter. The cultivation and improvement of the country, therefore, which affords subsistence, must, necessarily, be prior to the increase of the town, which furnishes only the means of convenience and luxury.*[2]

He also believed that human beings preferred living in the country and would move there if they made sufficient money in the towns. Thus the 'natural order of things', was for the countryside to flourish, and then the towns to follow suit. 'Had human institutions, therefore, never disturbed the natural course of things, the progressive wealth and increase of towns would, in every political society, be consequential, and in proportion to the improvement and cultivation of the territory or country.'[3]

Another concern was that though entrepreneurs ought to prefer the security of manufacturing goods for use in their own country rather than in getting involved in highly risky foreign trade, and should prefer agriculture to trade, yet this 'normal' course was increasingly being perverted in eighteenth century Europe. For 'though this natural order of things must have taken

---

[1] Weber, **Cities**
[2] Smith, **Wealth**, I, 402
[3] Smith, **Wealth**, I, 404

place in some degree in every such society, it has, in all the modern states of Europe, been, in many respects, entirely inverted. The foreign commerce of some of their cities has introduced all their finer manufactures, or such as were fit for distant sale; and manufactures and foreign commerce together, have given birth to the principle improvements of agriculture.'[4] In fact Glasgow was a prime example of the reversal of this 'natural' order, and hence to be castigated, since its wealth was principally based, like that of Holland, on long-distance trade - in particular, as we have seen, the tobacco and other trades with the West Indies and the Southern States of America, and on slavery.

This was closely linked to Smith's ambivalent attitude to merchants and manufacturers. On the one hand they were the focus for the first development of commercial capitalism, of liberty, and of the subduing of violence through the spread of wealth, and as such they are the heroes of his story. On the other hand he had no illusions about their benevolence. They had emerged by complete chance out of the stand-off between feudal lords and kings. As Dugald Stewart summarized Smith's position, the emergence of commercial centres 'took their rise, not from any general scheme of policy, but from the private interests and prejudices of particular orders of men.' This 'state of society, however, which at first arose from a singular combination of accidents, has been prolonged much beyond its natural period, by a false system of Political Economy, propagated by merchants and manufacturers, a class of individuals whose interest is not always the same with that of the public...' In other words, they had become too powerful - oligarchic and monopolistic and guild bound. Thus 'By means of this system, a new set of obstacles to the progress of national prosperity has been created.'[5]

---

4 Smith, **Wealth**, I, 405-6
5 Stewart, **Works**, X, 61

In particular, Smith was alluding to trade restrictions based on one his main, the mercantilist philosophy. 'The false system of Political Economy which has been hitherto prevalent, as its professed object has been to regulate the commercial intercourse between different nations, has produced its effect in a way less direct and less manifest, but equally prejudicial to the states that have adopted it.'[1] Thus the uneven development of the three components - agriculture, manufacture and trade, had led to the development of what Smith called the 'Commercial' or 'Mercantile' System or what we call Mercantilism. The two main methods of enriching a nation under this system were

> *restraints upon importation, and encouragements to exportation. Part of these expedients, he observes, have been dictated by the spirit of monopoly, and part by a spirit of jealousy against those countries with which the balance of trade is supposed to be disadvantageous. All of them appear clearly, from his reasonings, to have a tendency unfavourable to the wealth of the nation which imposes them.*[2]

Thus Smith felt that a good deal of the independent power of towns and their inhabitants was a beneficial accident in the West, but that the development was going too far towards trade monopolies and sectional interests.

※※※

In considering the problem of why England's wealth had 'insensibly' crept up and continued to grow, one key, Smith believed, lay in the social structure. His model of the economy and society is extremely 'modern'; it is not based on the usual **Ancien Regime** structure of a number of legally separate

---

1 Stewart, **Works**, X, 61, summarizing Smith's view.
2 Stewart, **Works**, X, 61

'estates' of nobility, peasantry, clergy and bourgeois, who exchange goods and services. It is split into 'three different orders of people...those who live by rent...by wages...by profit. These are the three great, original and constituent orders of every civilized society'.[3] They are the landlords, wage-labourers and employers of our modern capitalist state. It is clear from his analysis that he built this model up on the basis of his observations of how English society worked.

When trying to explain why England was so successful, he considered its geographical advantages, agreeing that it is 'perhaps as well fitted by nature as any large country in Europe, to be the seat of foreign commerce...'[4] He also pointed out that its legal code was favourable to commerce: 'in reality there is no country in Europe, Holland itself not excepted, of which the law is, upon the whole, more favourable to this sort of industry...'[5] But the geographical and legal advantages were less important than one other; 'what is of much more importance than all of them, the yeomanry of England are rendered as secure, as independent, and as respectable as law can make them.'[6] In other words, it is the curious position of what roughly might be called 'the middle class' that is crucial.

Smith asks rhetorically, what would the position of England have been if it 'had left the yeomanry in the same condition as in most other countries of Europe?'[7] He believed that 'Those laws and customs so favourable to the yeomanry, have perhaps contributed more to the present grandeur of England, than all their boasted regulations of commerce taken

---

3 Smith, **Wealth**, I, 276
4 Smith, **Wealth**, I, 442.
5 Smith, **Wealth**, I, 442.
6 Smith, **Wealth**, I, 443
7 Smith, **Wealth**, I, 443.

together.'¹ For their position and status was very different in England. 'Through the greater part of Europe the yeomanry are regarded as an inferior rank of people, even to the better sort of tradesmen and mechanics...'² There is consequently little investment by townsmen in the countryside, he believed, except in England, Holland and Berne in Switzerland.

As to why the yeomanry should be so powerful and prosperous, Smith's answer seems to be that in England, above all, the property law was such that they had private property and security of tenure. Even leases are more secure than elsewhere.

> *In England, therefore, the security of the tenant is equal to that of the proprietor. In England besides a lease for life of forty shillings a year value is a freehold, and entitles the lessee to vote for a member of parliament; and as a great part of the yeomanry have freeholds of this kind, the whole order becomes respectable to the landlords on account of the political considerations which this gives them. There is, I believe, no-where in Europe, except in England, any instance of the tenant building upon the land of which he had no lease, and trusting that the honour of his landlord would take no advantage of so important an improvement...The law which secures the longest leases against successors of every kind is, so far as I know, peculiar to Great Britain.³*

These differences were at least several centuries old. Whereas in France in the eighteenth century, Smith had been told that five-sixths of the whole kingdom was still held by some form of older share-cropping agreement, the **metayer**, such tenures 'have been so long in disuse in England that at present I know no English name for them'.⁴

---

1 Smith, **Wealth**, I, 415.
2 Smith, **Wealth**, I, 418.
3 Smith, **Wealth**, I, 415.
4 Smith, **Wealth**, I, 413-4.

These were differences in social structure which were reflected in the various colonies of France, Spain, England and other European countries. Thus he felt that 'the political institutions of the English colonies have been more favourable to the improvement and cultivation' of the New World than those of Continental countries. One of the central differences was that of alienability of land. In the continental colonies, the land was held as family property, in English colonies as an alienable commodity. Thus he described the differences, whereby in English colonies 'the tenure of the lands, which are all held by free socage, facilitates alienation', whereas in Spanish and Portuguese colonies 'what is called the right of Majorazzo takes place in the succession of all those great estates to which any title of honour is annexed. Such estates go all to one person, and are in effect entailed and unalienable...', while in French colonies, 'if any part of an estate, held by the noble tenure of chivalry and homage, is alienated, it is, for a limited time, subject to the right of redemption, either by the heir of the superior or by the heir of the family...which necessarily embarrass alienation.'[5] Thus the English system would tend to create a mass of middling folk, and the Continental systems would re-create the great divide between nobility and peasantry of the homeland.

Smith noted that 'In none of the English colonies is there any hereditary nobility.' There is a difference of esteem, but not of law; 'the descendant of an old colony family is more respected than an upstart of equal merit and fortune: but he is only more respected, and he has no privileges by which he can be troublesome to his neighbours'.[6] Indeed, he argues, it is a feature of the commercial states of which both old and new

---

5 Smith, **Wealth**, II, 83-4
6 Smith, **Wealth**, II, 98.

England were examples, that 'riches...very seldom remain long in the same family'.[1] The 'common law of England, indeed, is said to abhor perpetuities' and hence entails were in England 'more restricted than in any other European monarchy'.[2]

Smith's picture of eighteenth century England and New England is of modern commercial societies. The empire was created to provide buyers for English goods. 'To found a great empire for the sole purpose of raising up a people of customers, may at first sight appear a project fit only for a nation of shopkeepers. It is, however, a project altogether unfit for a nation of shopkeepers; but extremely fit for a nation whose government is influenced by shopkeepers.'[3] Smith assumes that such a mentality is very ancient.

Another part of the virtuous circle which Smith detected was that countries which were growing wealthier could afford greater taxes. 'Easy taxes' were one of his **desiderata** of course, but most civilizations had experienced the reverse; as they became wealthier, the separation of the classes grew, defence became more expensive and that condition which he had noted in China of a vast mass of miserably poor, with heavy rents and taxes, and a small group of very rich, tended to occur. He advocated the reverse. His first principle of taxation was equality. 'The subjects of every state ought to contribute towards the support of the government, as nearly as possible, in proportion to their respective abilities; that is, in proportion to the revenue which they respectively enjoy under the protection of the state.'[4] Secondly the taxation must be certain - that is to say predictable and not arbitrary. 'The time of payment, the manner of payment, the quantity to be paid, ought all to be

---

1 Smith, **Wealth**, I, 440.
2 Smith, **Wealth**, I, 409-10.
3 Smith, **Wealth**, II, 129.
4 Smith, **Wealth**, II, 350

clear and plain to the contributor, and to every other person.'[5] The arbitrary power of tax gatherers was disastrous.

Thirdly, 'Every tax ought to be levied at the time, or in the manner, in which it is most likely to be convenient for the contributor to pay it.'[6] Finally, it should be economically collected, as little as possible being siphoned off in the collection. Here he was describing a world not only of 'easy' taxes, but of a form of taxation to which the Dutch and English were accustomed, but certainly not those living in almost every other agrarian civilization in history. The powerful middle class and weak aristocratic interests were, of course, one of the bulwarks against the normal tendency towards unequal, unpredictable, inconvenient and uneconomical methods.

Smith had developed an aversion to unfair and arbitrary taxation early in his writings. In his lectures he had pointed out 'Whatever policy tends to raise the market price above the naturall one diminishes publick opulence and naturall wea<l>th of the state…Hence it is evident that all taxes on industry must diminish the national opulence as they raise the market price of the commodities.'[7] Yet the merchants were usually too weak to be able to do anything about it. 'All taxes upon exportation and importation of goods also hinder commerce. Merchants at first were in so contemptible a state that the law, as it were, abandoned them, and it was no matter what they obliged them to pay.'[8] All 'fiddling' with the natural order of things was unhelpful, in either a negative or positive way. 'Whatever breaks this naturall balance by giving either an extraordinary discouragement by taxes and duties, or [by] an extraordinary

---

5   Smith, **Wealth**, II, 350
6   Smith, **Wealth**, II, 351
7   Smith, **Jurisprudence**, 362
8   Smith, **Jurisprudence**, 529

encouragement by bounties or otherwise, tends to hurt the naturall opulence.'[1]

The security and fairness of the tax system was one consequence of the stability of the political system. Smith was very aware that random violence, whether of war, civil war, feuding or even arbitrary justice, would stifle tendencies towards commercial activity. Thus he believed that 'A man must be perfectly crazy who, where there is tolerable security, does not employ all the stock which he commands, whether it be his own or borrowed of other people, in some one or other...'[2] On the other hand, capital would become frozen during political insecurity.

> *In those unfortunate countries, indeed, where men are continually afraid of the violence of their superiors, they frequently bury and conceal a great part of their stock, in order to have it always at hand to carry with them to some place of safety, in case of their being threatened with any of those disasters to which they consider themselves as at all times exposed. This is said to be a common practice in Turkey, in Indostan, and, I believe, in most other governments of Asia. It seems to have been a common practice among our ancestors during the violence of the feudal government.*[3]

Thus the development of 'opulence' depended on the building of a whole infrastructure of legal and quasi-legal protection. Contracts must be binding and enforceable. 'Another thing which greatly retarded commerce was the imperfection of the law with regard to contracts, which were the last species of rights that sustained action, for originaly the law gave no redress for any but those concluded on the spot.'[4]

---

1 Smith, **Jurisprudence**, 365
2 Smith, **Wealth**, I, 301
3 Smith, **Wealth**, I, 301
4 Smith, **Jurisprudence**, 528

Tenure must be protected. 'As the tenants were continualy in danger of being turned out, they had no motive to improve the ground. This takes place to this day in every country of Europe except Brittain.'[5] Monopolies must be broken down. 'All monopolies and exclusive priviledges of corporations, for whatever good ends they were at first instituted, have the same bad effect.'[6]

One form of constraint on freedom which he noted, particularly in early studies, came not from the State but from the family. Smith explained the growing concern with property in the development from hunter-gatherers to settled pastoralists. 'In the age of hunters there could be no room for succession as there was no property. Any small things as bows, quiver etc. were buried along with the deceased; they were too inconsiderable to be left to an heir. In the age of shepherds, when property was greatly extended, the goods the deceased had been possessed of were too valuable to be all buried along with him.'[7] Once such valuable property occurred it tended to belong to the kinship group. In the 'age of shepherds', the respect for the family and blood line was particularly strong. 'We see many instances of the vast respect paid to descent amongst the Tartars and Arabs. Every one of these can trace themselves, at least they pretend to do so, as far back as Abraham.'[8]

Yet, as he had himself witnessed in the Scottish Highlands, as the clanship system of the 'shepherds' gave way to the new commercialized economy, the power of kinship declined. 'Regard for remote relations becomes in every country less and less, according as this state of civilization has been longer and

---

5   Smith, **Jurisprudence**, 524
6   Smith, **Jurisprudence**, 529
7   Smith, **Jurisprudence**, 39
8   Smith, **Jurisprudence**, 216

more completely established.'¹ Although the loss in martial spirit and warmth was to be lamented, this did increase the opportunities for the individual to keep the fruit of his or her own labour and hence encourage industriousness.

The extreme form of the break with the family could be seen in the spread of the use of last wills and testaments, and the possibility of exclusion of certain family members from the inheritance. Smith was puzzled by the emergence of this means of disposal. 'There is no point more difficult to account for than the right we conceive men to have to dispose of their goods after their death.'² He continued to wonder 'how is it that a man comes to have a power of disposing as he pleases of his goods after his death. What obligation is the community under to observe the directions he made concerning his goods now when he can have no will, nor is supposed to have any knowledge of the matter.'³ He realized that 'In the savage nations of Asia and Africa testamentary succession is unknown; the succession is intirely settled; a man's estate goes always to his nearest male relations, without his having the power of disposing, by any deed to take place after his death, of the smallest subject.'⁴

Yet something very odd and 'individualistic' had emerged in the medieval west, sometime in the period between the collapse of the Roman Empire and the tenth century. 'The German nations which overran Europe had no notion of testamentary succession; every inheritance was divided amongst the children; the only people amongst them (after the introduction of Christianity) who had any such idea were the clergy.'⁵ It was

---

1 Smith, **Moral**, 327
2 Smith, **Jurisprudence**, 63
3 Smith, **Jurisprudence**, 63
4 Smith, **Jurisprudence**, 65
5 Smith, **Jurisprudence**, 68

thus natural for Smith to argue, as others have done since, that it was the Christian clergy who introduced this device in order to encourage people to leave their property to the church.[6] 'As the clergy were the introducers of testamentary succession, so they were reckond the most proper persons to judge of it, as being best skilled...'[7] It was now possible for wealth to accumulate by the selection of heirs and bypassing the rights of the family at large.

This was a general feature, which was made even more powerful in western Europe, and particularly England, through an institution of which Smith clearly disapproved, namely primogeniture. He argued that the right of individual inheritance by the first born male was a technique introduced to overcome the independency of the great allodial estates, and the 'inconveniencies attending divisions of such estates.'[8] Thus 'this method of succession, so contrary to nature, to reason, and to justice, was occasioned by the nature of feudall government.'[9]

The other form of embedded, birth-given, control over the individual was slavery. Here again Smith noted a progression from almost universal slavery to its gradual elimination. This was both a cause and a consequence of economic growth. He noted first that even in the 1760s, slavery was very widespread. 'We are apt to imagine that slavery is entirely abolished at this time, without considering that this is the case in only a small part of Europe; not remembering that all over Moscovy and all the eastern parts of Europe, and the whole of Asia, that is, from Bohemia to the Indian Ocean, all over Africa, and the

---

6 See Goody, **Family**
7 Smith, **Jurisprudence**, 68
8 Smith, **Jurisprudence**, 56
9 Smith, **Jurisprudence**, 49

greatest part of America, it is still in use.'[1] He noted a paradox, that slavery became increasingly unacceptable as 'wealth' and equality developed more generally. 'We may observe here that the state of slavery is a much more tollerable one in <a> poor and barbarous people than in a rich and polished one.'[2]

The real puzzle was why an institution which was based on a powerful human drive came to be abolished at all.

Slavery therefore has been universall in the beginnings of society, and the love of dominion and authority over others will probably make it perpetuall. The circumstances which have made slavery be abolished in the corner of Europe in which it now is are peculiar to it, and which happening to concurr at the same time have brought about that change.[3]

His answer seems to have been that slavery went against the interests and ethics of the King and the Church, both of which had an interest in direct, free, relations with all the citizens or believers in a country. As the power of King and Church grew, so slavery was abolished. 'In Scotland, England, the authority of the king and of the church have been both very great; slavery has of consequence been abolished.'[4]

※※※

It is often alleged that Smith advocated a weak state. This is a half-truth. In fact what he suggested was that the State should both be strong, as a defence against sectional interests, but also not interfere too much. Ideally the State should be like a referee or umpire - able to punish or even expel, but not actually involved in the everyday contests and exchanges that led to wealth creation.

---

1 Smith, **Jurisprudence**, 181
2 Smith, **Jurisprudence**, 182
3 Smith, **Jurisprudence**, 187
4 Smith, **Jurisprudence**, 189

He believed that it had been private activities and not state interference which had led to the growth of England's wealth over time.

> *In the midst of all the exactions of government, this capital has been silently and gradually accumulated by the private frugality and good conduct of individuals, by their universal, continual, and uninterrupted effort to better their own condition. It is this effort, protected by law and allowed by liberty to exert itself in the manner that is most advantageous, which has maintained the progress of England towards opulence and improvement in almost all former times, and which, it is to be hoped, will do so in all future times.*[5]

He believed that the ideal situation would be that 'Every man, as long as he does not violate the laws of justice, is left perfectly free to pursue his own interest his own way, and to bring both his industry and capital into competition with those of any other man, or order of men.'[6] In order to effect and support this system of 'natural liberty'

> *the sovereign has only three duties to attend to; three duties of great importance, indeed, but plain and intelligible to common understandings: first, the duty of protecting the society from the violence and invasion of other independent societies; secondly, the duty of protecting, as far as possible, every member of the society from the injustice or oppression of every other member of it, or the duty of establishing an exact administration of justice; and, thirdly, the duty of erecting and maintaining certain public works and certain public institutions, which it can never be for the interest of any individual, or small number of individuals, to erect and maintain; because the profit could never repay the expenc to any individual or small number of individuals, though it may frequently do much more than repay it to a great society.*[7]

---

5   Smith, **Wealth**, I, 367

6   Smith, **Wealth**, II, 208

7   Smith, **Wealth**, II, 208-9

Thus Smith realized that the duties were 'of great importance', but they were specific and limited, and included the provision of public, utilities and infrastructure, and a public system of justice.

Smith likewise saw both the merits but also the dangerous absolutist tendencies of organized religion. In an interesting but little quoted chapter on the 'Institutions for Religious Instruction' he gave a brief account, no doubt heavily influenced by the views of his friend David Hume, of the dangers and advantages of religious enthusiasm.

He noted the danger of politicians taking sides in sectarian squabbles, summarizing his argument in the heading 'If politics had never called in the aid of religion, sects would have been so numerous that they would have learnt to tolerate each other.'[1] He pointed to the good example of Pennsylvania, where though the Quakers were the most numerous, 'the law in reality favours no one sect more than another, and it is there said to have been productive of this philosophical good temper and moderation.'[2] He saw that tolerance developed out of the productive balance and tension of different religious positions. Citing Hume's ideas almost verbatim, he wrote:

> *In every civilized society, in every society where the distinction of ranks has once been completely established, there have been always two different schemes or systems of morality current at the same time; of which the one may be called the strict or austere; the other the liberal, or, if you will, the loose system. The former is generally admired and revered by the common people: the latter is commonly more esteemed and adopted by what are called people of fashion.*[3]

Religious sects, he argued, usually began with the austere, puritanical, position of the country people. They may take

---

1 Smith, **Wealth**, II, 314
2 Smith, **Wealth**, II, 315
3 Smith, **Wealth**, II, 315-6

this to extreme lengths so that 'in small religious sects morals are regular and orderly and even disagreeably rigorous and unsocial.'[4] This puritanical attitude can be ameliorated by encouraging such sectarians to broaden their minds with science and philosophy, painting, poetry, music, dancing and such things.

Smith then considers the dangers of an Established Church, which tends again to become too powerful. Combined with the growing wealth of the State this made it 'exceedingly formidable.'[5] The extreme example of this tendency was, of course, the Papacy,

> *In the state in which things were through the greater part of Europe during the tenth, eleventh, twelfth, and thirteenth centuries, and for some time both before and after that period, the constitution of the church of Rome may be considered as the most formidable combination that ever was formed against the authority and security of civil government, as well as against the liberty, reason, and happiness of mankind, which can flourish only where civil government is able to protect them.*[6]

What then brought down this great and increasing power, as potent a threat as the feudal lords? Smith suggests the same force as before, namely the growth of commercial wealth, and in exactly the same way. In other words, it was not destroyed from outside, but corrupted by greed from inside.

> *The gradual improvements of arts, manufactures, and commerce, the same causes which destroyed the power of the great barons, destroyed in the same manner, through the greater part of Europe, the whole temporal power of the clergy. In the produce of arts, manufacturers, and commerce, the clergy, like the great barons, found something for*

---

4 Smith, **Wealth**, II, 317

5 Smith, **Wealth**, I, 323

6 Smith, **Wealth**, II, 325

> *which they could exchange their rude produce, and thereby discovered the means of spending their whole revenues upon their own persons, without giving any considerable share of them to other people. Their charity became gradually less extensive, their hospitality less liberal or less profuse. Their retainers became consequently less numerous, and by degrees dwindled away altogether. The clergy too, like the great barons, wished to get a better rent from their landed estates, in order to spend it, in the same manner, upon the gratification of their own private vanity and folly. But this increase of rent could be got only by granting leases to their tenants, who thereby became in a great measure independent of them. The ties of interest, which bound the inferior ranks of people to the clergy, were in this manner gradually broken and dissolved.*[1]

This internal corruption had weakened the Established Churches well before the Reformation. But that movement was the final blow. The enthusiasm of the Reformers was supported by the puritanical zeal of ordinary people, and thus 'enabled sovereigns on bad terms with Rome to overturn the Church with ease.'[2]

The form of government in England, whereby the Lutherans formed a weak link with the Crown, 'was from the beginning favourable to peace and good order, and to submission to the civil sovereign.'[3] In Scotland the Calvinist system had been less successful because the 'Election by the people gave rise to great disorders', with a fanatical clergy and factions and controversies.[4] This period of disorder was ended by the various early eighteenth century acts which helped to diminish the factionalism. Thus by his own time, Smith could comment that 'There is scarce perhaps to be found any where in Europe a more learned, decent, independent, and respectable set of men, than the greater part of the presbyterian

---

[1] Smith, **Wealth**, II, 325-6
[2] Smith, **Wealth**, II, 328
[3] Smith, **Wealth**, II, 330
[4] Smith, **Wealth**, II, 331

clergy of Holland, Geneva, Switzerland and Scotland.'[5] Thus Church and State were reasonably balanced, and neither was either willing or able to halt the progress towards the general improvements in trade, manufacture and wealth, in Smith's meaning of that word.

---

5 Smith, **Wealth**, II, 333

FOUR

From Predation to Production

Living within a few miles of the Highland Line, and having narrowly avoided the Scots clan-based army in 1745, Adam Smith was deeply aware of how fragile and original was the kind of commercial order which he saw in England. Thus when he wrote that all that was needed was 'peace, easy taxation and a due administration of justice' he not only selected three political conditions but must have been fully aware that such conditions were incredibly difficult to fulfil. He was not making a statement about how **easy** the 'natural course' of opulence was, but how difficult. How then had these conditions emerged, in particular in England? This is one of the trickiest of questions, the relations between power and wealth. The powers of predation were bound to be stronger and more desirable than the powers of production. So how did wealth creation ever continue in any sustained and prolonged way?

The question could be put in the form, how did violence gradually ebb away? Smith has several lines of argument to explain this, but the central, and somewhat circular one, is that people were gradually 'civilized' by increasing wealth - or as Samuel Johnson put it 'There are few ways in which a man can be more innocently employed than in getting money.'[1] Here is the argument, incorporating a certain amount of questionable history, based on Smith's knowledge of England and France.

---

1 Quoted in Oxford Dictionary of Quotations, 208

At the start, the world approximated Marc Bloch's 'dissolution of the State' feudalism, with powerful lords and their bands of retainers and castles, as Smith must have witnessed in his youth in the Highlands. The centre was very weak. The King in those 'ancient times' was

> *little more than the greatest proprietor in his dominions, to whom, for the sake of common defence against their common enemies, the other great proprietors paid certain respects. To have enforced payment of a small debt within the lands of a great proprietor, where all the inhabitants were armed and accustomed to stand by one another, would have cost the king, had he attempted it by his own authority, almost the same effort as to extinguish a civil war. He was, therefore, obliged to abandon the administration of justice through the greater part of the country, to those who were capable of administering it; and for the same reason to leave the command of the country militia to those whom that militia would obey.*[2]

Thus the great proprietors, Smith thought, had the power to raise troops, execute justice and so on before and after the Norman Conquest of England. Gradually the imposition of feudal law after the twelfth century, led to some reigning in of the over-mighty barons. 'The introduction of the feudal law, so far from extending, may be regarded as an attempt to moderate the authority of the great allodial lords. It established a regular subordination, accompanied with a long train of services and duties, from the king down to the smallest proprietor.'[3] Yet, even after the introduction of feudal subordination, he believed, 'the king was as incapable of restraining the violence of the great lords as before. They still continued to make war according to their own discretion, almost continually upon one another, and very frequently

---

2 Smith, **Wealth**, I, 435
3 Smith, **Wealth**, I, 436

upon the king; and the open country still continued to be a scene of violence, rapine, and disorder.'[1]

So what turned the tide of violence if it was not the political system? Here, returning to that theme of the civilizing effect of commerce, Smith brings forward his explanation.

> *But what all the violence of the feudal institutions could never have effected, the silent and insensible operation of foreign commerce and manufactures gradually brought about. These gradually furnished the great proprietors with something for which they could exchange the whole surplus produce of their lands, and which they could consume themselves without sharing it either with tenants or retainers. All for ourselves, and nothing for other people, seems, in every age of the world, to have been the vile maxim of the masters of mankind.*[2]

Here again Smith was writing exactly about his own, post-Culloden, experience as he watched the Scottish clan lords dismiss their followers and turn their lands over to sheep and other more profitable commodities with which they could raise the cash to leave the Highlands and live in the cities of southern Scotland or England.

> *In a country where there is no foreign commerce, nor any of the finer manufactures, a man of ten thousand a year cannot well employ his revenue in any other way than in maintaining, perhaps, a thousand families, who are all of them necessarily at his command. In the present state of Europe, a man of ten thousand a year can spend his whole revenue, and he generally does so, without directly maintaining twenty people, or being able to command more than ten footmen not worth the commanding.*[3]

Thus the retainers were sacked and the lords became consumers in a commercial society.

---

1 Smith, **Wealth**, I, 437
2 Smith, **Wealth**, I, 437
3 Smith, **Wealth**, I, 437-8

Likewise the tenants were reduced.

Farms were enlarged, and the occupiers of land, notwithstanding the complaints of depopulation, reduced to the number necessary for cultivating it, according to the imperfect state of cultivation and improvement in those times. By the removal of the unnecessary mouths, and by exacting from the farmer the full value of the farm, a greater surplus, or what is the same thing, the price of a greater surplus, was obtained for the proprietor, which the merchants and manufacturers soon furnished him with a method of spending upon his own person in the same manner as he had done the rest.[4]

Although Smith does not explicitly say so, he is both describing what he saw happening before him in the Highland clearances and projecting it backwards as a model for what he thought must have happened in England in the later middle ages as a feudal society gave way to a commercial one.

This revolution was an unintended and accidental event. No-one was aware of what was happening, partly because the change happened in England over a long period. Hence, as the marginal heading put it, 'A revolution was thus insensibly brought about.' What this revolution was, and its accidental nature, is summarized by Smith thus.

A revolution of the greatest importance to the public happiness, was in this manner brought about by two different orders of people, who had not the least intention to serve the public. To gratify the most childish vanity was the sole motive of the great proprietors. The merchants and artificers, much less ridiculous, acted merely from a view to their own interest, and in pursuit of their own pedlar principle of turning a penny wherever a penny was to be got. Neither of them had either knowledge or foresight of that great revolution which the folly of the one, and the industry of the other, was gradually bringing about.[5]

---

4   Smith, **Wealth**, I, 438-9
5   Smith, **Wealth**, I, 440

All this was, of course, topsy turvy and hence progress was much slower than it should be. For 'It is thus that through the greater part of Europe the commerce and manufactures of cities, instead of being the effect, have been the cause and occasion of the improvement and cultivation of the country.'[1] This 'being contrary to the natural course of things', was 'necessarily both slow and uncertain.'[2] Yet it had happened - just. What should really happen was shown by developments in North America. 'Compare the slow progress of those European countries of which the wealth depends very much upon their commerce and manufactures, with the rapid advances of our North American colonies, of which the wealth is founded altogether in agriculture.'[3]

The process was complex and contained many feed-back loops. As the wealth increased, so the legal framework upon which Smith believed flourishing commercialism must be based grew stronger. A particularly important factor was the increasing separation of the executive and the judiciary, in other words an impartial judiciary which will protect citizens from that arbitrary arrogance of power to be found in most agrarian and totalitarian Empires. Here again, Smith thought the key was growing wealth.

The idea of the importance of 'due administration of justice' as one of the keys to capitalism was expanded by Smith.

> *When the judicial is united to the executive power, it is scarce possible that justice should not frequently be sacrificed to, what is vulgarly called, politics. The persons entrusted with the great interests of the state may, even without any corrupt views, sometimes imagine it necessary to sacrifice to those interests the rights of private man. But upon the impartial administration of justice depends the liberty of every individual, the sense*

---

1 Smith, **Wealth**, I, 440

2 Smith, **Wealth**, I, 441

3 Smith, **Wealth**, I, 441

> *which he has of his own security. In order to make every individual feel himself perfectly secure in the possession of every right which belongs to him, it is not only necessary that the judicial should be separated from the executive power, but that it should be rendered as much as possible independent of that power. The judge should not be liable to be removed from his office according to the caprice of that power. The regular payment of his salary should not depend upon the good-will, or even upon the good oeconomy of that power.*[4]

This crucial change came about because, as certain nations became wealthier, the amount of business increased, and hence the famous division of labour applied here also.

> *The separation of the judicial from the executive power seems originally to have arisen from the increasing business of the society, in consequence of its increasing improvement. The administration of justice became so laborious and so complicated a duty as to require the undivided attention of the persons to whom it was entrusted. The person entrusted with the executive power, not having leisure to attend to the decision of private causes himself, a deputy was appointed to decide them in his stead.*[5]

Smith believed that this had happened in the Roman Empire, and again in medieval and early modern England. It is an ingenious idea, but does not fully accord with what happened in the Turkish, Habsburg, Russian or Chinese Empires. Obviously growing wealth is only part of the answer.

Another ingenious circularity lies in the effect of growing wealth on the propensity to violence. Basically the argument is that people are too busy to be violent, and find it more convenient to follow the principle of the division of labour and buy off the threat of violence by hiring others to police their borders. This leads to an over-all decline in war-like feelings on the part of the majority of the population. Smith

---

[4] Smith, **Wealth**, II, 243-4
[5] Smith, **Wealth**, II, 243

put it in an evolutionary way thus.

> *A shepherd has a great deal of leisure; a husbandman, in the rude state of husbandry, has some; an artificer or manufacturer has none at all. The first may, without any loss, employ a great deal of his time in martial exercises; the second may employ some part of it; but the last cannot employ a single hour in them without some loss, and his attention to his own interest naturally leads him to neglect them altogether. Those improvements in husbandry too, which the progress of arts and manufactures necessarily introduces, leave the husbandman as little leisure as the artificer. Military exercises come to be as much neglected by the inhabitants of the country as by those of the town, and the great body of the people becomes altogether unwarlike.*[1]

Smith's thesis was

> *confirmed by universal experience. In the year 1745 four or 5 thousand naked unarmed Highlanders took possession of the improved parts of this country without any opposition from the unwarlike inhabitants. They penetrated into England and alarmed the whole nation, and had they not been opposed by a standing army they would have seized the throne with little difficulty. 200 years ago such an attempt would have rouzed the spirit of the nation.*[2]

This was specifically the result of the effects of the division of labour and commerce. 'Another bad effect of commerce is that it sinks the courage of mankind, and tends to extinguish martial spirit. In all commercial countries the division of labour is infinite, and every ones thoughts are employed about one particular thing.'[3]

Smith's ambivalence about this process is shown even more clearly when he wrote 'The defence of the country is therefore committed to a certain sett of men who have nothing else ado;

---

1 Smith, **Wealth**, II, 219-220

2 Smith, **Jurisprudence**, 540-1

3 Smith, **Jurisprudence**, 540

and among the bulk of the people military courage diminishes. By having their minds constantly employed on the arts of luxury, they grow effeminate and dastardly.'[4] This was a 'bad' effect because it meant that almost automatically, as a nation became richer, it became a prey to others. They were both more attractive and more vulnerable. It was a situation which was obvious to Smith.

> *That wealth, at the same time, which always follows the improvements of agriculture and manufactures, and which in reality is no more than the accumulated produce of those improvements, provokes the invasion of all their neighbours. An industrious, and upon that account a wealthy nation, is of all nations the most likely to be attacked; and unless the state takes some new measures for the public defence, the natural habits of the people render them altogether incapable of defending themselves.*[5]

He expanded this theme at length in his lectures on jurisprudence, with particular reference to the Roman Empire. He showed how

> *when the whole people comes to be employed in peacefull and laborious arts, 1 out of 100 only can go, that is, about 1000, which would be no more than a poor city guard and could do nothing against an enemy; nor even 4 or 5000. So that the very duration of the state and the improvements naturally going on at that time, every one applying himself to some usefull art, and commerce, the attendant on all these, necessarily undo the strength and cause the power to vanish of such a state till it be swallowed up by some neighbouring state.*[6]

This forced a state to turn to using either the dregs of society, or paid mercenaries.

---

4 Smith, **Jurisprudence**, 540

5 Smith, **Wealth**, II, 220

6 Smith, **Jurisprudence**, 230-31

> *Thus then when arts were improved, those who in the early times of the state had alone been trusted would not now go out, and those who before had never engaged in battle were the only persons who made up the armies, as the proletarii or lowest class did in the later periods of Rome. The armies are diminished in number but still more in force. This effect commerce and arts had on all the states of Greece. We see Demosthenes urging them to go out to battle themselves, instead of their mercenaries which their army then consisted of; nor of these were there any considerable number. Whenever therefore arts and commerce engage the citizens, either as artizans or as master trades men, the strength and force of the city must be very much diminished.*[1]

This was the fate of all small enclaves like the Greek city states. 'All states of this sort would therefore naturally come to ruin, its power being diminished by the introduction of arts and commerce, and its territory, and even its very being, being held on a very slender tack after the military art was brought to tolerable perfection, as it had nothing to hope for when once defeated in the field.'[2] There was a vicious circle. The very force that led to wealth led to ruin. 'Here improvement in arts and cultivation unfit the people from going to war, so that the streng<th> is greatly diminished and it falls a sacrifice to some of its neighbours. This was the case of most of the republicks of Greece. Athens in its later time could not send out the 5th part of what it formerly did.'[3] A classic case was also provided by the fate of the Italian city states. 'The Italian republicks in the same manner paid subsidies to some of the neighbouring chiefs who engaged to bring 10,000 or 5000 horse, which were then chiefly in request, for their protection. Every small state had some of these in their pay. This soon brought on their ruin'[4]

---

1 Smith, **Jurisprudence**, 232
2 Smith, **Jurisprudence**, 233
3 Smith, **Jurisprudence**, 235
4 Smith, **Jurisprudence**, 243

Their weakness was increased by changes in military technology. With improved weaponry it became impossible to defend a city, for

> *there is an other improvement which greatly diminishes the strength and security of such a state; I mean the improvement of the military art. The taking of cities was at fir<s>t a prodigious operation which employed a very long time, and was never accomplished but by stratagem or blockade, as was the case at the Trojan war. A small town with a strong wall could hold out very well against its enemies.*[5]

If such a city State tried an alternative tactic, that is imperial expansion, it ran into the problems which Montesquieu had outlined. Smith believed that the lust for domination and power was very strong.

> *The Love of domination and authority over others, which I am afraid is naturall to mankind, a certain desire of having others below one, and the pleasure it gives one to have some persons whom he can order to do his work rather than be obliged to persuade others to bargain with him, will for ever hinder this from taking place.*[6]

As Rome expanded, so the army and its generals became more powerful.

> *Of all the republicks we know, Rome alone made any extensive conquests, and became thus in danger from its armies under the victorious leaders. But the same thing was feared and must have happend at Carthage had the project of Hanniball succeded, and he made himself master of Italy.*[7]

The classic instance was, of course, Caesar. The behaviour of the Senate in Rome

---

5   Smith, **Jurisprudence**, 232
6   Smith, **Jurisprudence**, 192
7   Smith, **Jurisprudence**, 236

affronted Caesar; he had recourse to his army who willingly joind him, and by repeated victories he became Dictator for ever. The remains of the same victorious army afterwards set Antony and Augustus, and at last Augustus alone, on the throne. And the same will be the case in all conquering republicks where ever a mercenary army at the disposall of the generall is in use.[1]

How could a country or confederacy of states escape from this vicious circle? They could not rely on international law.

In war, not only what are called the laws of nations are frequently violated, without bringing (among his own fellow-citizens, whose judgments he only regards) any considerable dishonour upon the violator; but those laws themselves are, the greater part of them, laid down with very little regard to the plainest and most obvious rules of justice.[2]

Smith's only hope was that the incessant warfare would become milder. Earlier wars had been fought out of wander-lust and in a pure predatory fashion - the search for booty; modern commercial nations fought in order to secure or increase their territory. 'A polished nation never undertakes any such expeditions. It never makes war but with a design to enlarge or protect its territory; but these people make war either with design to leave their own habitations in search of better, or to carry off booty.'[3] This change of motive reduced the destructive element in war. 'The same policey which makes us not so apt to go to war makes us also more favourable than formerly after an entire conquest. Anciently an enemy forfeited all his possessions, and was disposed of at the pleasure of the conquerors. It was on this account that the Romans had often to people a country anew and send out colonies. It is

---

1 Smith, **Jurisprudence**, 234
2 Smith, **Moral**, 218
3 Smith, **Jurisprudence**, 220

not so now. A conquered country in a manner only changes masters.'[4] The change was only at the very top. 'They may be subjected to new taxes and other regulations, but need no new people. The conqueror generally allows them the possession of their religion and laws, which is a practice much better than the ancient.'[5]

This milder form of conquest was accompanied by a less bloody form of warfare, thanks to modern weapons. Adam Smith knew the difference between Highlanders armed with claymores, and English troops with their muskets. 'Modern armies too are less irritated at one another because fire arms keep them at a greater distance. When they always fought sword in hand their rage and fury were raised to the highest pitch, and as they were mixed with one another the slaughter was vastly greater.'[6] All of this change, however, depended on neighbouring societies all being 'enlightened' and commercial. Until the fifteenth century or so, western Europe had been the prey of powerful Mongol armies. Only recently had the new form of 'commercial' warfare become dominant - and destructive though it was, it was less disastrous than that which China and western European nations had faced for thousands of years. Yet Smith was still left with the puzzle of that crucial movement from small, vulnerable, commercial city-states, to large but not too large nation-states which somehow combined commercial affluence with the power to defend themselves. The answer lay in English history.

---

4 Smith, **Jurisprudence**, 550
5 Smith, **Jurisprudence**, 550
6 Smith, **Jurisprudence**, 550

We saw that Montesquieu singled out England as his extreme case of liberty and Smith was to do the same, also emphasizing its wealth. The problem was to account for its success, for, as Campbell and Skinner note, 'Smith believed that England was really a special case, and that she alone had escaped from absolutism.'[1] In his **Lectures on Jurisprudence** he gave a narrative of how this had happened.

He believed that after the collapse of the Roman Empire two forms of government succeeded each other. At first from about 400 to 800 A.D. there was a form of 'allodial government' where 'the lords held their lands of no one, but possessed them as their own property.' Then 'the feudall government arose about 400 years afterwards, about the 9th century.'[2] This emerged largely out of a new power relationship between the lords and the king. 'When any of the great allodial lords was in danger of being oppressed by his neighbours, he called for protection from the king against them. This he could not obtain without some consideration he should perform to him. A rude and barbarous people who do not see far are very ready to make concessions for a temporary advantage.'[3] The new arrangement was as follows. 'For these considerations the king gave up all his demesne lands, and the great allodiall lords their estates, to be held as feuda, which before had been held as munera. A tenent who held a feu was very near as good as property. He held it for himself and his heirs for ever. The lord had the dominium directum, but he had the dominium utile which <? was> the principle and most beneficial part of

---

1 Campbell and Skinner, **Smith**, 118

2 Smith, **Jurisprudence**, 244

3 Smith, **Jurisprudence**, 250

property.'[4] The chain of feudal links was thus set up. 'Those services secured his protection, and in this manner the inferior allodial lords came to hold of the great ones, and these again of the king; and the whole thus held of him either mediately or immediately, and the king was conceived to have the dominium directum of all the lands in the kingdom.'[5] This was a change which 'happened in the whole of Europe about the 9, 10, 11st centuries.'[6]

All the lands 'fell under the immediate jurisdiction of the lords or of the king, who administered judgment in them either by himse<l>f or by judges sent for that purpose.'[7] One side effect of this was to protect the lowest tenants. They avoided the fate of all previous agricultural workers, namely slavery, for though they were 'unfree',

> *They were however in a much better condition than the slaves in ancient Greece or Rome. For if the master killed his villain he was liable to a fine; or if he beat him so as that he died within a day he was also liable to a fine; these, tho small priviledges, were very considerable and shewd great superiority of condition if compared with that of the old slaves.*[8]

Thus up to about the eleventh century, all of western Europe was fairly uniform. After this Smith began to detect a growing divergence. Over continental Europe the power of the ruler increased. Only in England did this not happen. Everywhere powerful rulers overthrew

> *the democraticall part of the constitution and establish an aristocraticall monarchy. This was done in every country excepting England, where*

---

4 Smith, **Jurisprudence**, 250
5 Smith, **Jurisprudence**, 251
6 Smith, **Jurisprudence**, 252
7 Smith, **Jurisprudence**, 254
8 Smith, **Jurisprudence**, 255

> *the democraticall courts subsisted long after and usually did business; and at this day the county court, tho it has not been used of a long time, is nevertheless still permitted by law.*[1]

The nobility, which could have put up a resistance to the absolutist tendency, were crushed, a necessary precursor to liberty, but leading to a dangerous void. 'We see too that this has always been the case; the power of the nobles has always been brought to ruin before a system of liberty has been established, and this indeed must always be the case. For the nobility are the greatest opposers and oppressors of liberty that we can imagine.'[2]

They were also weakened because of the growing commercial prosperity - a process Smith had observed with the Highland chiefs. Speaking of a typical lord or laird, he wrote,

> *When luxury came in, this gave him an opportunity of spending a great deal and he therefore was at pains to extort and squeeze high rents from them. This ruind his power over them. They would then tell him that they could not pay such a rent on a precarious chance of possession, but would consent to it if he would give them long possessions of them; which being convenient for both is readily agreed to; and they became still more independent when in the time of Henry 2d these leases came to sustain action at law contra quemcumque possessorem. Thus they lost a man for 10 or 5 sh., which they spent in follies and luxury. The power of the lords in this manner went out, and as this generally happened before the power of the commons had come to any great pitch, an absolute government generally followed.*[3]

This was a necessary stage between feudalism and modern liberty.

---

1 Smith, **Jurisprudence**, 258

2 Smith, **Jurisprudence**, 264

3 Smith, **Jurisprudence**, 262.

> Whereas every one is in danger from a petty lords, who had the chief power in the whole kingdom. The people therefore never can have security in person or estate till the nobility have been greatly crushed. Thus therefore the government became absolute, in France, Spain, Portugal, and in England after the fall of the great nobility.[4]

Smith had noted a difference between England and the Continent early on, and continues this theme from time to time up to the later fifteenth century. Thus he argues that the English were often able to gain some freedom and power when their rulers were needing money to fight wars abroad.

> *The people we see were always most free from their severall burthens when the profits arising from them to the state were most necessary for its support. We see accordingly that those which are most favourable to liberty are those of martiall, conquering, military kings. Edward the 1st and Henry the 4th, the two most warlike of the English kings, granted greater immunities to the people than any others.*[5]

He explained why this should be so.

> *There are severall reasons for this, as 1st, they of all others depended most on the goodwill and favour of their people; they therefore court it greatly by all sorts of concessions which may induce them to join in their enterprizes. Peaceable kings, who have no such occasion for great services or expensive expedition<s>, [and] therefore less courted their love and favour. 2dly, it soon became a rule with the people that they should grant no subsidies till their requests were first granted.*[6]

Thus the loss of English interest in their French claims in the fifteenth century, according to Smith, was a disaster. The nobility were weakened in the Wars of the Roses. 'They had been massacred by Edward 4th in his battles with Henry the

---

4   Smith, **Jurisprudence**, 264
5   Smith, **Jurisprudence**, 260
6   Smith, **Jurisprudence**, 260.

6th; afterwards in various insurrections and disputes for the crown.'¹ Under the Tudors they sunk into a form of absolutism.

> *In the last lecture I observd how the nobility necessarily fell to ruin as soon as luxury and arts were introduced. Their fall everywhere gave occasion to the absolute power of the king. This was the case even in England. The Tudors are now universally allowed to have been absolute princes. The Parliament at that time, instead of opposing and checking the measures they took to gain and support their absolute power, authorized and supported them. Henry the 7th was altogether an absolute monarch...²*

This narrative left Smith with a problem. All of Europe was now absolutist. How then in the less than two hundred years between Henry VII and the later seventeenth century had England, alone, shed absolutism? Smith put forward two arguments. The first was the rash activity of Elizabeth I. A thing which

> *contributed to the diminution of the kings authority, and to render him still more weak, was that Elizabeth in the end of her reign, forseeing that she was to have no sucessors of her own family, was at great pains to gain the love of the nation, which she had generally done, and never inclined to lay on taxes which would she knew be complaind of; but she chose rather to sell the demesne lands, which were in her time alltogether alienated. James 1st and Charles had in this manner no revenue, nor had they a standing army by which they could extort any money or have other influence with the people.³*

Smith explained how absolutism increased over continental Europe. But the

> *situation and circumstances of England have been altogether different. It was united at length with Scotland. The dominions were then entirely*

---

1   Smith, **Jurisprudence**, 262
2   Smith, **Jurisprudence**, 264
3   Smith, **Jurisprudence**, 266

> *surrounded by the sea, which was on all hands a boundary from its neighbours. No foreign invasion was therefore much to be dreaded. We see that (excepting some troops brought over in rebellions and very impoliticly as a defence to the kingdom) there has been no foreign invasion since the time of Henry 3d. ... The Scots however frequently made incursions upon them, and had they still continued seperate it is probable the English would never have recovered their liberty. The Union however put them out of the danger of invasions. They were therefore under no necessity of keeping up a standing army; they did not see any use of necessity for it.*[4]

He contrasted this with the position of continental nations.

> *In other countries, as the feudall militia and that of a regular one which followd it wore out, they were under a necessity of establishing a standing army for their defense against their neighbours. The arts and improvement of sciences puts the better sort in such a condition that they will not incline to serve in war. Luxury hinders some and necessary business others.*[5]

Thus the English and French diverged through a combination of Elizabeth's profligacy and the security of England's island position after union with Scotland.

> *We see in France that Henry the fourth kept up generally a standing army of betwixt 20 and 30,000 men; this, tho small in comparison of what they now keep up, was reckoned a great force, and it was thought that if France could in time of peace maintain that number of men it would be able to give law to Europe; and we see it was in fact very powerfull. But Britain had no neighbours which it could fear, being then thought superior to all Europe besides. The revenues of the king being very scanty, and the desmesnes lands, the chief support of the kings, being sold, he had no more money than was necessary to maintain the dignity and grandeur of the court. From all these, it was thought unnecessary as well as inconvenient and useless to establish a standing army.*[6]

---

4   Smith, **Jurisprudence**, 265

5   Smith, **Jurisprudence**, 265

6   Smith, **Jurisprudence**, 266

The result was that when the Civil War was fought, Charles lost. Again, when James II tried to impose his Catholic will, he could not do so. Thus, for largely accidental and fortuitous reasons, England's political history took a different turn.

Smith was not content to leave the story here, however. Following closely some of the arguments of Montesquieu, he tried to outline the institutional structures which now guaranteed the balance of power and the liberty and security of the people of Britain, which was the foundation, as he thought, of their growing wealth and power.

There was firstly England's parliament. By the middle of the eighteenth century,

> *So far is the king from being able to govern the kingdom without the assistance of Parliament for 15 or 16 years, as Chas. 1st did, that he could not without giving offence to the whole nation by a step which would shock every one, maintain the government for one year without them, as he has no power of levying supplies. In this manner a system of liberty has been established in England before the standing army was introduced; which as it was not the case in other countries, so it has not been ever establishd in them.*[1]

The system was now firmly entrenched. 'Liberty thus established has been since confirmed by many Acts of Parliament and clauses of Acts. The system of government now supposes a system of liberty as a foundation. Every one would be shocked at any attempt to alter this system, and such a change would be attended with the greatest difficulties.'[2] The House of Commons was powerful enough to control the royal power and the power of ministers. 'Another article which secures the liberty of the subjects is the power which the Commons have of impeaching the kings ministers of mal-administration, and that tho it had

---

1 Smith, **Jurisprudence**, 269
2 Smith, **Jurisprudence**, 271

not visibly encroached on liberty.'³ Furthermore, 'The House of Commons also has the sole judgement in all controverted elections, and is on them very nice and delicate, as their interest leads them to preserve them as free as can be had.'⁴

Yet the Commons themselves were restrained from the corruption of power by periodic elections. 'The frequency of the elections is also a great security for the liberty of the people, as the representative must be carefull to serve his country, at least his constituents, otherwise he will be in danger of losing his place at the next elections.'⁵ In summary, 'These laws and established customs render it very difficult and allmost impossible to introduce absolute power of the king without meeting with the strongest opposition imaginable.'⁶ All this had occurred through a balance of forces. Smith rejected both Hobbes and Locke's ideas of the social contract arising from a voluntary agreement. As he explained, he had 'endeavoured to explain to you the origin and something of the progress of government. How it arose, not as some writers imagine from any consent or agreement of a number of persons themselves to submit themselves to such or such regulations, but from the natural progress which men make in society.'⁷

The other great protection, in suggesting which Smith again partly followed Montesquieu, was the English Common Law tradition. One aspect was a free and independent judiciary, judges who were separate from the royal or even the parliamentary power.

> *One security for liberty is that all judges hold their office[r]s for life and are intirely independent of the king. Every one therefore is tried by a free*

---

3   Smith, **Jurisprudence**, 272
4   Smith, **Jurisprudence**, 274
5   Smith, **Jurisprudence**, 273
6   Smith, **Jurisprudence**, 274
7   Smith, **Jurisprudence**, 207

> *and independent judge, who are als<o> accountable for their conduct. Nothing therefore will influ<en>ce them to act unfairly to the subject, and endang<er> the loss of a profitable office and their reputation also; nothing the king could bestow would be an equivalent. The judge and jury have no dependance on the crown.*[1]

He expanded this a little later, by pointing out that the judges themselves were limited in their power.

> *I had observed an other thing which greatly confirms the liberty of the subjects in England. - This was the little power of the judges in explaining, altering, or extending or correcting the meaning of the laws, and the great exactness with which they must be observed according to the literall meaning of the words, of which history affords us many instances.*[2]

Part of this limitation, which prevented yet another danger, that of an arbitrary justice, was due to the healthy rivalry between different courts - providing reasonable competition in justice.

Another thing which tended to support the liberty of the people and render the proceedings in the courts very exact, was the rivalship which arose betwixt them. The Court of Kings Bench, being superior to the Court of Com. Pleas and having causes frequently transferred to them from that court, came to take upon it to judge in civill causes as well as in criminall ones, not only after a writ of error had been issued out but even immediately before they had passed thro the Common Pleas.'[3]

Smith had already drawn attention to the independence of jurors, but he elaborated this further as a key protection of the citizen against the State, and also against the power of judges.

---

1 Smith, **Jurisprudence**, 271
2 Smith, **Jurisprudence**, 275
3 Smith, **Jurisprudence**, 280

> *Another thing which curbs the power of the judge is that all causes must be try'd with regard to the fact by a jury. The matter of fact is left intirely to their determination. - Jurys are an old institution which formerly were in use over the greater part of the countries in Europe, tho they have now been laid aside in all countries, Britain excepted.*[4]

Great care was taken to maintain their independence and reliability. 'Nothing can be more carefull and exact than the English law in ascertaining the impartiality of the jurers. They must be taken from the county where the persons live, from the neghbourhood of the land if it be a dispute of property, and so in other cases.'[5]

Thus an independent, but not too powerful, judge, and an independent jury seemed together 'to be a great security of the liberty of the subject.' As he explained to his Scottish students, in England,

> *One is tried here by a judge who holds his office for life and is therefore independent and not under the influence of the king, a man of great integrity and knowledge who has been bred to the law, is often one of the first men in the kingdom, who is also tied down to the strict observance of the law; and the point of fact also determined by a jury of the peers of the person to be tried, who are chosen from your neighbourhood, according to the nature of the suit, all of whom to 13 you have the power of challenging.*[6]

The final protection was **Habeas Corpus,** which is 'also a great security against oppression, as by it any one can procure triall at Westminster within 40 days who can afford to transport himself thither.'[7] This prevented arbitrary imprisonment without trial.

---

4   Smith, **Jurisprudence**, 283
5   Smith, **Jurisprudence**, 284
6   Smith, **Jurisprudence**, 284-5
7   Smith, **Jurisprudence**, 272

Smith's account of the English development is intriguing and scholarly. He clearly knew the literature and wrote with authority. Yet there is something of a contradiction in it. On the one hand his account of political power suggests that England like continental Europe went through an absolutist phase. The difference was that it occurred much later, lasted for a much shorter period (c.1475-1580) and was overturned, whereas the absolutist governments grew ever more powerful in France, Spain, Germany and elsewhere.

On the other hand, on the legal side he gives a sketch of much more continuity and of the preservation of a high degree of protection against the power of the State. He summarizes his finding in this area as follows.

> *There seems to be no country in which the courts are more under regulation and the authority of the judge more restricted. The form of proceedings as well as the accuracy of the courts depends greatly on their standing. Now the courts of England are by far more regular than those of other countries, as well as more ancient. The courts of England are much more ancient than those of France or Scotland.*[1]

It was one of several contradictions in his portrayal of English history which make his account suggestive about the events after about 1600, but less accurate for the earlier period.

❈❈❈

There are a number of reasons for looking on Adam Smith as an optimist. He believed, like Pope, that whoever stood behind the visible world, had intended mankind to be happy. 'The happiness of mankind, as well as of all other rational creatures, seems to have been the original purpose intended by the Author of Nature when

---

1 Smith, **Jurisprudence**, 286-7

he brought them into existence.'² In general such an 'Author' had been successful. 'Take the whole earth at an average, for one man who suffers pain or misery, you will find twenty in prosperity and joy, or at least in tolerable circumstances.'³

This view was confirmed by the history of the fairly recent past. Firstly, he could see that progress had been made over most of Europe since the fifteenth century and that his own Scotland was, in parts, becoming very much richer. Violence was on the retreat. As Eric Roll summarizes his Enlightenment optimism here, 'Fundamentally, he, like most later liberal philosophers, was an optimist. The social evils which he saw around him he ascribed to past mistakes of government...Smith's whole work implied great faith in the possibility of freeing the state from the incubus of individual or class influence. Once this emancipation was achieved the natural harmony would be manifest to all.'⁴ The very basis of his work was the belief that an 'Inquiry into the Nature and Causes of the Wealth of Nations' was both possible, and that having found such causes, nations could take appropriate and remedial action.

A particular cause for optimism was his belief that the balance between production and predation had changed. A cause for quiet confidence was the fact that wealth and general virtue were connected. As Stewart noted of his findings, 'the most wealthy nations are those where the people are the most laborious, and where they enjoy the greatest degree of liberty.'⁵ They were also characteristically more equal societies, with a large and mobile middling group and the decline of serfdom and aristocracy. The trouble was that when such societies had emerged anywhere else before, as in the Italian city states, they

---

2   Smith, **Moral**, 235.
3   Smith, **Moral**, 197.
4   Roll, **Economic**, 152
5   Stewart, **Works**, X, 58

had quickly been destroyed by envious neighbours. The forces of destruction or predation had always been too strong for the pockets of wealth to resist.

As Adam Smith reflected on the last major contest in British soil between predation and production, the clash between the warlike clans and the mercenary army of the English at Culloden in 1745, it must have been very obvious that the balance had shifted. How and why this had happened, being strongly related to technological changes, is outlined by Smith as follows.

He noted that over time the cost of defence increased as nations became wealthier.

> *The first duty of the sovereign, therefore, that of defending the society from the violence and injustice of other independent societies, grows gradually more and more expensive, as the society advances in civilization. The military force of the society, which originally cost the sovereign no expence either in time of peace or in time of war, must, in the progress of improvement, first be maintained by him in time of war, and afterwards even in time of peace.[1]*

This cost was increased still further by modern weapons technology. The battle of Culloden was decided by fire power, by superior technology, more than anything else.

> *The great change introduced into the art of war by the invention of fire-arms, has enhanced still further both the expence of exercising and disciplining any particular number of soldiers in time of peace, and that of employing them in time of war. Both their arms and their ammunition are become more expensive. A musket is a more expensive machine than a javelin or a bow and arrows; a cannon or a mortar than a balista or a catapulta. The powder, which is spent in a modern review, is lost irrecoverably, and occasions a very considerable expence.[2]*

---

1 Smith, **Wealth**, II, 230

2 Smith, **Wealth**, II, 230

The effect of this was to favour the rich, rather than those who had previously ruled the earth, the warlike. Rich shopkeepers could now easily defeat poor Highlanders.

> *In modern war the great expence of fire-arms gives an evident advantage to the nation which can best afford that expence; and consequently, to an opulent and civilized, over a poor and barbarous nation. In ancient times the opulent and civilized found it difficult to defend themselves against the poor and barbarous nations. In modern times the poor and barbarous find it difficult to defend themselves against the opulent and civilized. The invention of firearms, an invention which at first sight appears to be so pernicious, is certainly favourable both to the permanency and to the extension of civilization.*[3]

Thus Smith believed that one of the negative feed-back mechanisms which had constantly operated in the past, bringing down the Roman Empire, leaving civilizations vulnerable to Mongol invasions, even keeping his native Scotland in thrall, had at last been overcome. Wealth and military power were for the first time united with liberty and equality.

This is the optimistic side. Yet at another level, Smith, like the successor classical economists Malthus and Ricardo, was a pessimist - and for exactly the same reasons. As he looked around him he saw that progress was possible - up to a limit, but then seemed to hit some invisible barrier or ceiling. China was the great example; that mighty civilization, wealthier than Europe, seemed to have been 'stationary' since the time of Marco Polo. India was not 'progressing'. The shape of things to come was shown by Holland, which had been 'stationary', if not declining, for nearly a hundred years. France, previously very wealthy, had also been 'stationary' for about a hundred years or so. Italy had only recovered the level of her pre-1500

---
3   Smith, **Wealth**, II, 230-1

eminence. Spain and Portugal were 'going backwards'. Only England, still with some way to reach Holland's level, and tiny Scotland and the under-populated spaces of North America, were progressing rapidly.

E.A. Wrigley has summarized an aspect of Smith's pessimism; 'his view of the prospects of growth in general induced him to discount the possibility of a prolonged or substantial improvement in real wages, and to fear that the last state of the labourer would prove to be worse than the first, a view that was reinforced by his anticipation of some of the arguments to which Malthus was later to give the classic formulation.'[1] Smith could not see what would in fact happen. '...Smith himself was unaware of the immense changes already in train when the **Wealth of nations** was written. Indeed, the implications of the arguments he used would rule out the possibility of rapid and sustained economic growth. The great revolution of which he wrote was an economic revolution... but it was not an **industrial revolution** as that term has come to be used.'[2]

What Smith accurately described was a closed system which, in the case of most of the European countries and China, had reached the limits of possible progress. He had observed a fact which Wrigley endorses, which is that 'In their essential nature traditional economies were negative feedback systems. At some point the growth process itself provoked changes which causes growth to decelerate and grind to a halt. Success in a particular round of growth implied difficulty at a later stage.'[3]

Smith gave three major reasons why there was no possibility of continuous long-term growth and why a country such as

---

1 Wrigley, 'Two Kinds', 99-100
2 Wrigley, **People**, 58
3 Wrigley, 'Two Kinds', 115

Holland had just about reached the limits. One of these was that the rate of profit would continually fall. This mechanism was demonstrated by the history of Holland.

> *In a country which had acquired its full complement of riches, where in every particular branch of business there was the greatest quantity of stock that could be employed in it, as the ordinary rate of clear profit would be very small, so the usual market rate of interest which could be afforded out of it, would be so low as to render it impossible for any but the very wealthiest people to live upon the interest of their money. All people of small or middling fortunes would be obliged to superintend themselves the employment of their own stocks. It would be necessary that almost every man should be a man of business, or engage in some sort of trade. The province of Holland seems to be approaching near to this state. It is there unfashionable not to be a man of business. Necessity makes it usual for almost every man to be so, and custom every where regulates fashion.*[4]

England would soon reach this plateau and then, like Holland, became stuck in one form of the high-level equilibrium trap.[5]

A second mechanism, which partly stemmed from the first, was the law of diminishing marginal returns, particularly in agriculture. This was more famously and explicitly enunciated by Malthus and Ricardo, but it was also obvious to Smith. Put simply, new land produces a good harvest, but as demands continue it produces less, and the use of marginal lands, or the application of extra labour brings decreasing returns. The principle of the division of labour had temporarily overcome part of this problem, but the marginal returns on the division of labour also began to reach a limit. Mankind was trapped on a treadmill which required more and more effort for less and less returns. As

---

4 Smith, **Wealth**, I, 108
5 For further discussion of the rate of declining profit, see Wrigley, **People**, 29-32

Wrigley notes, the restraints which seemed to be 'permanent and ineradicable' in Smith's world were that land was the source of all wealth, and that energy was limited to what could be obtained directly from the sun, wind and water.[1]

The third law that trapped mankind was that of population. In a direct anticipation of Malthus, Smith explained how the history of agrarian societies showed that 'men, like all other animals, naturally multiply in proportion to the means of their subsistence'[2] Thus whenever the wealth of a nation increased, and in particular if this wealth was shared by the mass of the population through higher real wages, the population would increase to absorb the increase. This is the point which Smith stresses in both volumes of his book. In the first he notes that, as he puts it in the heading, 'High wages increase population'. 'The liberal reward of labour, therefore, as it is the effect of increasing wealth, so it is the cause of increasing population. To complain of it, is to lament over the necessary effect and cause of the greatest public prosperity.'[3] Or in a more expanded way

> *The liberal reward of labour, by enabling them to provide better for their children, and consequently to bring up a greater number, naturally tends to widen and extend those limits. It deserves to be remarked too, that it necessarily does this as nearly as possible in the proportion which the demand for labour requires. If this demand is continually increasing, the reward of labour must necessarily encourage in such a manner the marriage and multiplication of labourers, as may enable them to supply that continually increasing demand by a continually increasing population.*[4]

---

1 Wrigley, 'Two Kinds', 105
2 Smith, **Wealth**, I, 163.
3 Smith, **Wealth**, I, 90
4 Smith, **Wealth**, I, 89

The law of supply and demand works with population as with anything else. Thus 'the demand for men, like that for any other commodity, necessarily regulates the production of men.'[5]

The danger was even greater because poverty in itself did not necessarily limit population growth. 'Poverty, though it no doubt discourages, does not always prevent marriage. It seems even to be favourable to generation. A half-starved Highland woman frequently bears more than twenty children, while a pampered fine lady is often incapable of bearing any...' What poverty did do, he thought, was to kill off large numbers of infants: 'in the Highlands of Scotland it is not uncommon for a mother who has borne twenty children not to have two alive.'[6] Thus, if the standard of living and medical care of the poor increased markedly, the problem of population growth would be even greater. Mankind was caught in the Malthusian trap. Every short term gain would lead to a larger problem in the future.

Thus placing ourself in Adam Smith's world as he sat beside the Firth of Forth slowly compiling the **Wealth of Nations** in the years before 1776, we can see how he must have felt clearly both grounds for measured short-term optimism and long-term pessimism. The 'natural' path to increased opulence was there to be taken if the mainly political obstacles could be removed. Everyone could, in theory, reach the level of the Dutch. But then people were trapped on a high-level plateau. Although they were not so vulnerable to external destruction and predation, there were reasons for suspecting that having reached the plateau, the only path was downwards. Growing population, the monopolistic tendencies of greedy merchants or even farmers, the ambitions of the State, the ambitions of

---

5   Smith, **Wealth**, I, 89
6   Smith, **Wealth**, I, 88

the Church, any or all of these could shatter the precarious balance of forces.

This is ultimately Smith's message. Although there was a 'natural tendency' for the selfish and competitive drives of human beings to lead to the growth of wealth if appropriate conditions were provided, continuous, unlimited, growth was impossible. The growth in the past had been the unintended consequence of a set of accidents - outcomes of conflicts and oppositions which had against all the odds led to gradual growth. Many had strayed from the path - Eastern Europe, later much of Southern Europe, China and India. Even France was in doubt and Germany is hardly mentioned. Only on an outlying tip of north-west Europe, and in the New World, was conspicuous growth still occurring. It is not surprising, therefore, that Adam Smith, like Malthus and Ricardo 'unanimously and explicitly denied the possibility of the change now regarded as its [industrial revolution] most important single feature, and perhaps as its great redeeming feature - the substantial and largely continuous rise in the standard of living that it has occasioned.'[1] Mankind was trapped at a high level equilibrium.

It was also trapped in another way. A number of commentators have pointed out that Smith anticipates Marx concerning some of the disastrous side-effects of the new industrial-capitalism which he saw emerging around him.[2] He had observed that alongside the growing wealth, even in the richest parts of one of the richest countries in the world, England, there was increasing misery, although part of this was self-inflicted.

---

1 Wrigley, 'Two Kinds', 103

2 For example the essays by R.L.Heilbronner and E.G.West in Skinner and Wilson, **Essays on Adam Smith**

> *Accordingly we find that in the commercial parts of England, the tradesmen are for the most part in this despicable condition; their work through half the week is sufficient to maintain them, and through want of education they have no amusement for the other but riot and debauchery. So it may very justly be said that the people who clothe the whole world are in rags themselves.*[3]

This was no accident, for it rose from the very essence of the new division of labour which was the motor of change. He had noticed that 'It is remarkable that in every commercial nation the low people are exceedingly stupid. The Dutch vulgar are eminently so, and the English are more so than the Scotch. The rule is general, in towns they are not so intelligent as in the country, nor in a rich country as in a poor one.'[4] This was not because of some innate inferiority, but because of the crippling effects of a life making pin heads. Partly there was the sheer pettiness and boredom of the activity.

> *Where the division of labour is brought to perfection, every man has only a simple operation to perform. To this his whole attention is confined, and few ideas pass in his mind but what have an immediate connection with it. When the mind is employed about a variety of objects it is some how expanded and enlarged, and on this account a country artist is generally acknowledged to have a range of thoughts much above a city one.*[5]

Partly it was because education was brushed aside in the rush to use the labour of children.

> *Another inconvenience attending commerce is that education is greatly neglected. In rich and commercial nations the division of labour, having reduced all trades to very simple operations, affords an opportunity*

---

3 Campbell and Skinner, **Smith**, 121

4 Smith, **Jurisprudence**, 539

5 Smith, **Jurisprudence**, 539

of employing children very young. In this country indeed, where the division of labour is not far advanced, even the meanest porter can read and write, because the price of education is cheap, and a parent can employ his child no other way at 6 or 7 years of age.[1]

He concluded, 'These are the disadvantages of a commercial spirit. The minds of men are contracted and rendered incapable of elevation, education is despised or at least neglected, and heroic spirit is almost utterly extinguished. To remedy these defects would be an object worthy of serious attention.'[2] It was a serious attention which Smith himself, unfortunately, was unable to provide. Indeed, since he did not fully appreciate the liberating effects of machinery, it was difficult, if not impossible, for him to see a way round these difficulties.

Thus both at the national and individual level, the 'wealth of nations' was tinged with failure. Mankind had not escaped from the treadmill of existence, even if the present condition in a few favoured nations was perhaps better than it had been since the descent from the 'original affluent society' of hunter-gathering.

In terms of Smith's solution to the riddle, he confirmed certain parts of the answer already suggested by Montesquieu. He noted the normal tendency to stasis, the beneficial effects of commerce, the difficulties caused by the size, homogeneity and rice cultivation in China, the dangers of conquest and war, the importance of English Common Law, the importance of a reasonable taxation system and secure investment opportunities, and the advantage of being an island.

New areas of the puzzle now filled in included the discussion of

---

1 Smith, **Jurisprudence**, 539-40

2 Smith, **Jurisprudence**, 541

the rise and effect of towns, of the middle class, the night watchman state and church. He put forward the theory that liberty emerges when sects fall out with each other and adds to this a description of the effects of commercial wealth on power. His account of the mechanism for the escape from violence through the growth of opulence is extremely suggestive. And his re-working of the theory of the division of labour provides some dynamic for the change. His account of English development adds detail to Montesquieu and re-enforces the importance of islandhood. Smith warned of the dangers of all monopolies of power, even those of producers and exchangers, he noted the role of the judiciary in safeguarding economic well-being and he noted the importance of the unification of England and Scotland. He even anticipated some of the negative effects of the division of labour and a commercial mentality on the morals and well-being of future generations.

Yet even when we add his formidable contribution to that of Montesquieu, the riddle is still unresolved. The fact that Smith was pessimistic about the future shows that he did not solve it. Part of the answer lay in the development of science and industrial technology which he only glimpsed. He was on the whole unaware of the power of the scientific revolution, that is the growth of new knowledge through the use of the experimental method, which provided the basis for the new manufacture of artifacts through the industrial process. Nor did he fully realize that the rapid growth of England was dependent on its position as part of a European network of knowledge. We might say that after the contributions of Montesquieu and Smith the solution was half complete. Like many operations, the relatively easier parts are done first. To fill in the last parts is the most difficult and it is indeed fortunate that in Tocqueville and Maitland we find thinkers fit for the task of adding some of the final pieces.[3]

---

3   See my books on Tocqueville and Maitland in this series

Bibliography

THE BIBLIOGRAPHY INCLUDES all works referred to in the text, except for those by Smith. His works are listed at the front of the work. All books are published in London, unless otherwise indicated.

The following abbreviations have been used.

ed. edited or editor
edn edition
eds. editors
Jnl. Journal
n.d. no date
tr. translated by
Univ. University

Campbell, R.H.& Skinner, A.S., **Adam Smith**, 1982.
Chamberlayne, E, **The Present State of England**, 19th impression, 1700
Elvin, Mark, **The Pattern of the Chinese Past**, 1973.
Farrer, J.A., **Adam Smith**, Altrincham, 1988.
Fay, C.R., **The World of Adam Smith**, Cambridge 1960.
Fitzgibbons, Athol, **Adam Smith's System of Liberty, Wealth and Virtue. The Moral and Political Foundations of the Wealth of Nations**, Oxford, 1995
Goody, Jack, **The Development of the Family and Marriage in Europe**, Cambridge, 1983
Hume, David, **The History of England, From the Invasion of Julius Caesar to the Revolution in 1688.** 8 vols, London, 1823.
Hume, David, **Essays, Literary, Moral and Political**, n.d. c.1870; Ward, Lock & Tyler reprint of 2 vols. 8vo edn.

Jones Peter & Skinner, Andrew S. (eds), **Adam Smith Reviewed**, Edinburgh, 1992.

Kames, Lord, **Sketches of the History of Man**, Basil (Basle), 1796.

Lux, Kenneth, **Adam Smith's Mistake**, 1990.

Macfarlane, Alan, **The Origins of English Individualism**, Oxford, 1978.

Macfarlane, Alan, **The Culture of Capitalism**, Oxford, 1987.

Mandeville, Bernard, **The Fable of the Bees**, ed. F.B.Kaye, 2 vols. Oxford, 1924. Mandeville, Bernard, **The Fable of the Bees**, ed. Phillip Harth, Penguin, 1970.

Meek, Ronald L. **Social Science and the Ignoble Savage**, Cambridge, 1976.

Meek, Ronald L. **Smith, Marx, & After**, 1977

Rae, John. **Life of Adam Smith** (1895), New York, 1965.

Richter, Melvin, 'Montesquieu', **Encyclopedia of the Social Sciences**, 2nd edn., 1968.

Ross, Ian Simpson. **The Life of Adam Smith**, Oxford, 1995.

Scott, William Robert, **Adam Smith as Student and Professor**, Glasgow, 1937.

Skinner, Andrew S, & Wilson, Thomas (eds), **Essays on Adam Smith**, Oxford, 1975.

Skinner, Andrew S, **A System of Social Science: Papers Relating to Adam Smith**, Oxford, 1979.

Stewart, Dugald. 'Biographical Memoirs of Adam Smith, LL.D.' in **Collected Works**, vol.X, Edinburgh, 1858.

Stocking, George W. 'Scotland as the Model of Mankind: Lord Kames' Philosophical View of Civilization' in **Toward a Science of Man; Essays in the History of Anthropology**, ed. Timothy Thoresen, Mouton, The Hague, 1975.

Wilson, Thomas and Skinner, Andrew S., **The Market and the State: Essays in Honour of Adam Smith**, Oxford, 1976.

Wrigley, E.A., **Continuity, Chance and Change; The**

character of the industrial revolution in England, Cambridge, 1993.

Wrigley, E.A., **Peoples, Cities and Wealth; the Transformation of Traditional Society**, Oxford, 1992.

ALAN MACFARLANE

Encounters with Major Thinkers

THIS BOOK IS part of a series of short studies which explain the contribution of a number of major thinkers who have been concerned with wide problems in the social sciences.

In each book I explore the ways a thinker, or thinkers, try to understand the birth and growth of the modern world. They have each looked outside their own time and culture to try to find the deeper laws and tendencies, the accidents and patterns, which have governed the development of societies and civilizations.

In particular I have been interested to explore the relationship between the life and the work of each thinker, how their experiences and work methods shaped their theoretical contributions.

The series is also being published in Chinese.

EXPLORE THE SERIES

1. Montesquieu and the Making of the Modern World
2. Adam Smith and the Making of the Modern World
3. Thomas Malthus and the Making of the Modern World
4. Alexis de Tocqueville and the Making of the Modern World
5. Fukuzawa Yukichi and the Making of the Modern World
6. F.W. Maitland and the Making of the Modern World
7. Four Approaches to the Making of the Modern World

Made in the USA
Columbia, SC
30 October 2024